P9-DCD-273

RELIGIONS OF
STAR TREK

RELIGIONS OF
STAR TREK

Ross S. Kraemer

William Cassidy

Susan L. Schwartz

A Member of the Perseus Books Group

Copyright © 2001 by Westview Press, A Member of the Perseus Books Group

Westview Press books are available at special discounts for bulk purchases in the United States by corporations, institutions, and other organizations. For more information, please contact the Special Markets Department at The Perseus Books Group, 11 Cambridge Center, Cambridge MA 02142, or call (617) 252-5298.

Published in 2001 in the United States of America by Westview Press, 5500 Central Avenue, Boulder, Colorado 80301–2877, and in the United Kingdom by Westview Press, 12 Hid's Copse Road, Cumnor Hill, Oxford OX2 9JJ

Find us on the World Wide Web at www.westviewpress.com

Text design by *Brent Wilcox*
Set in 11-point Berkeley Book by Perseus Publishing Services

A CIP catalog record for this book is available from the Library of Congress.
ISBN 0-8133-6708-5

The paper used in this publication meets the requirements of the American National Standard for Permanence of Paper for Printed Library Materials Z39.48–1984.

10   9   8   7   6   5   4   3   2   1

CONTENTS

v

PREFACE

One of life's interesting little moments became the genesis for this book. In the fall of 1994, Susan Schwartz, a professor of Asian religions at Muhlenberg College, and Bill Cassidy, a specialist in the religions of the ancient Mediterranean at Alfred University, were in need of a third paper for a panel on Star Trek and the teaching of religion to be held at a regional meeting of the American Academy of Religion in Boston. Ross Kraemer, also a scholar of religions of the ancient Mediterranean who was then teaching at the University of Pennsylvania, shared Susan and Bill's fascination with Star Trek and its many explorations of intergalactic religions and religious themes. With a small amount of arm-twisting, Susan prevailed upon Ross to join the panel.

We first explored some of the uses of Star Trek in the teaching of religious studies, knowing that many of our students thought Star Trek was a productive vehicle for studying religion. To our surprise and delight, the room was soon packed with a diverse group of religion professors fired up about the prospect of an academic session on Star Trek and the study of religion. Afterward we were approached by one of the many editors who attend such meetings in search of new projects; with her encouragement, we began to envision a book on Star Trek and religion.

Writing it required some difficult choices. Star Trek's longevity and appeal over thirty-plus years have resulted in an extraordinary amount of material. There is now something approximating an "orthodox" canon: the TV episodes from the original *Star Trek* series, *Next Generation*, *Deep Space Nine*, *Voyager*, the nine feature films, and a library of authorized commentary (including novels, audio materials, and survey volumes with the Paramount imprimatur). There is also a huge amount of unauthorized commentary by fans and enemies in many media, as well as an electronic database almost too vast to be explored in one lifetime. Faced with this body of information, we have chosen to limit our analyses to the four TV series and the nine feature films. We did resort, occasionally, to the use of "unauthorized" episode guides. We also decided to set aside the fascinating question of fans who treat Star Trek as a religion of sorts.

Even within these limited parameters, however, there are inconsistencies on many issues, including religion. In fact, as we have discovered, there are sometimes inconsistencies between the episodes available on tape and official Paramount materials (such as differences in script). Recent Paramount publications provide data about events and characters that seem missing from the episodes themselves.

As we compiled sections of this book, swapped files and hard copy, ran up our phone bills on conference calls, and spent occasional weekends together rethinking and revising, we engaged the same issues time and again. A threshold issue was the appropriateness of writing a book about religion and Star Trek that treats more or less as a coherent whole the TV series and feature films, which were written, directed, produced, and acted by diverse persons over a period of thirty years. We knew that creator Gene Roddenberry and his successors at Paramount had envisioned Star Trek as cohesive and consistent, yet we easily identified inconsistencies and differences that intrigued us even as we struggled with our interpretations and analyses.

Ultimately, we reached a comfort level with this dilemma, as we face such challenges all the time in our profession. Like the diverse religions we study and teach, the Star Trek universe has changed over time and revealed glimpses of itself: new characters, newly divulged history, deities formerly untold, truths revealed, practices altered, and beliefs revised. All this is true of Earth-bound religions as well. Incredible richness and inconsistency go hand in hand along with the natural desire for uniformity underlying the vast diversity. Perhaps writing about Star Trek and religion appeals to us because the questions the series poses are so familiar.

As we began to develop this book, we knew we were not alone. Scholars in many fields—from physics to philosophy to psychology to literature—also use Star Trek as a vehicle to explore concepts, issues, and theories. Given that Star Trek is so enormously useful in teaching undergraduates, it's no surprise that others have written books on the phenomenon to make their disciplines more accessible.

Yet when we convened that first panel, the professional literature on our specific theme—Star Trek and religion—was almost nonexistent. During the intervening years, it has not exactly burgeoned, but it has grown little. And even though our analyses and interpretations were developed independently and thus do not engage others' views directly, some of our conclusions are consistent with the views of others, although our primary focus on the representation of religion has led us to devote entire chapters to topics others less fully consider, such as religious devotion and the existence of gods.

We hope that the results of our work will engage many fans of Star Trek. We have, for the most part, enjoyed it immensely. Our individual views about Star Trek and religion are generally in accord, but there are differences in our thinking and approaches. Chapters 1 and 5 are largely Ross Kraemer's work; Chapters 2 and 6, largely Bill Cassidy's; Chapters 3 and 4, largely Susan Schwartz's. The remainder was written by committee.

We would like to acknowledge Susan Worst for setting this process in motion. We would also like to thank Laura Parsons of Westview Press for her initial enthusiastic support of the project, as well as Sarah Warner for seeing it through to completion. Numerous academic departments dedicated to the study of religion provided opportunities to share ideas, both in the classroom and through public lectures, including Alfred University, Lehigh University, Muhlenburg College, Macalester College, Wesleyan University, Williams College, and the University of Pennsylvania; we thank them all.

We would also like to acknowledge a small but growing group of religious studies scholars who have come to view Star Trek as a fruitful area of inquiry and an instructive vehicle for teaching students about real, as well as imaginary, religion. We are particularly thankful to Julia Hardy, Brad Verter, and Sarah Schwarz for their critical readings of drafts along the way.

Finally, we thank our families, especially our children, for watching many Star Trek episodes with us all these years and for tolerating our insistence that in religion, as well as in many things, Star Trek is not just another TV series.

Introduction:
The Religions of Star Trek

In the classic episode "Who Mourns for Adonais?" from the
original *Star Trek* series, Captain James T.

Kirk, the charming,
youthful-looking leader of the Starship *Enterprise*, stands before an artificially fabricated Greek temple on some M-class
planet in the middle of the galaxy. There, he tells the real (and
not very amused) Greek god Apollo: "Mankind has no need
for gods. We find the one quite adequate." By the end of the
episode, it was all clear: Apollo, Athena, Zeus, and the rest of
the ancient Greek pantheon were powerful interstellar travelers who merely took advantage of the ignorance of the inhabitants of a relatively primitive planet several thousand years
earlier to set themselves up as the objects of adoration. Only
when those inhabitants evolved somewhat did they abandon
their worship of those false gods, who then departed, dejected
and starved for affection, to other realms of the universe. It
was corny, but the point was hard to miss: Ancient Greek religion was based on the real experiences of humans who lacked
sufficient knowledge to interpret them. And what of the casual

reference to the adequate "one?" Have Terrans in the twenty-third century abandoned their ancient polytheism for a true (or at least truer?) monotheism?

In the collective imagination of Star Trek, the religious landscape of the twenty-third and twenty-fourth centuries is characterized by abundant and diverse forms of extraterrestrial piety. Vulcans, Klingons, Bajorans, Ferengi, and myriad other galactic civilizations cherish and practice their indigenous religious traditions. Among humans (referred to as Terrans in this book), however, religion appears conspicuous by its absence. Still, in the fourth Star Trek TV series—*Voyager*—one Terran, Commander Chakotay, continues to adhere to twenty-fourth-century forms of the spiritual practices of his Native American ancestors. On the whole, however, there is little evidence of late-twentieth-century religions in the third millenium, whether Judaism, Christianity, Islam, Hinduism, Buddhism, New Age spirituality, or anything else.

Gene Roddenberry's original series, which was broadcast for three seasons (fall 1967 through spring 1970), had little positive to say about religion. Isolated exceptions can be noted: The origins of Christianity received relatively gentle treatment in "Bread and Circuses" (aired March 1968), a second-season show re-creating the emergence of Christianity in a technologically advanced version of ancient Rome, complete with gladiatorial contests on television. Thus, the fleeting allusion to Terran monotheism in "Who Mourns for Adonais?" (aired September 1967) should hardly be taken as an indicator of the *Enterprise*'s piety, any more than Uhura's wonderment in "Bread and Circuses" that the "sun" worshipped is really the "son" should be taken as evidence for crypto-Christians among the crew. In the Original Series, religion appears almost exclusively as an aspect of "the Other"—and usually the "primitive Other" at that.

In *Star Trek: The Next Generation*, which debuted twenty years after the Original Series (September 1987), religion and its themes became subtler and more complex. Beliefs and practices weren't only for caricatured primitives like the people of Vaal in "The Apple" but also for advanced cultures. Klingons, we found out, believe in everything from a dead warrior-king who will return someday (Kahless the Unforgettable) to two realms of the dead, Sto-Vo-Kor (for the honored dead) and Gre'thor (for the dishonored). The profit-obsessed Ferengi believe that after their bodies have been cremated and sold to the highest bidders their souls go to a Divine Treasury where they will be held accountable for their practice of the 285 Rules of Acquisition. A virtual parody, maybe, yet even in these brief glimpses, it demonstrates a coherence of social structures and religious beliefs and practices strikingly familiar to contemporary students of religion.

Many *Next Generation* episodes were concerned, at least implicitly, with religious themes. There were ongoing encounters—from the inaugural episode "Encounter at Farpoint" (aired September 1987) to the final episode "All Good Things. . . " (May 1994)—between the crew and the perplexing character known only as Q (part of the enigmatic Q Continuum), who possesses the critical Western divine attributes of omniscience and omnipotence yet receives none of the reverence and awe traditionally accorded the deity in Terran societies. There was the time Captain Jean-Luc Picard had to outwit a female figure claiming to be the demonic Ardra, who demanded payment in a Faustian bargain with the people of Ventax II in "Devil's Due" (aired February 1991). The prodigy

Ensign Wesley Crusher, considered by many fans as an irritating boy-wonder, became the disciple of a being known only as the Traveler. In a first-season *Next Generation* episode ("Where No One Has Gone Before," airdate October 26, 1987), this enigmatic figure saves the *Enterprise* from destruction at the cost of great personal suffering, almost unto death, evoking allusions to suffering saviors such as Jesus. In the final season, in "Journey's End" (aired March 1994) the Traveler returns to guide Wesley in a spiritual and bodily transformation that culminates in Wesley's departure from the *Enterprise* to attain new levels of existence and self-understanding. Although religious experiences seemed to be everywhere, Terran crew members of the *Enterprise* appear largely devoid of any connection to Terran religion.

Several Star Trek films, the first (*Star Trek The Motion Picture*) being produced in 1979, explicitly addressed religious themes: creation, death, and resurrection (*Star Trek II: The Wrath of Khan* [1982] and *Star Trek III: The Search for Spock* [1984]), the existence of God (*Star Trek V: The Final Frontier* [1989]), and tantalizing allusions to heaven and immortality (*Generations* [1994]). The 1999 film *Insurrection* took the stance that excessive technology is dangerous to the fabric of communal life and to the inner peace of individuals. The Ba'ku seem to evoke a kind of spirituality adapted from Eastern models. But because the majority of Star Trek films appeared largely in the years before the debut of *Next Generation*, the representations of religion in many of these films tended to fit more closely with the Original Series.

The two Star Trek spin-off series produced after Roddenberry's death at age 70 on October 24, 1991—*Deep Space Nine* (January 1993 to spring 1999) and *Voyager* (1995 to

2001)—paid direct attention to religion, beginning with the inaugural episodes. The very first episode of *Deep Space Nine*, "Emissary" (aired January 1993), centered on the complex religion of the inhabitants of the planet Bajor, around which Space Station Deep Space Nine orbits. Indeed, as we will explore at great length in several chapters of this book, *Deep Space Nine* ultimately became a startlingly intense religious drama centered around the role of the space station's commander (later captain), Benjamin Sisko, as the preordained emissary of Bajoran deities, known as the Prophets.

In its early episodes *Voyager*, too, directly engaged religious issues. The inaugural two-part episode, "Caretaker" (aired January 1995), dealt with a powerful being facing an extraordinary dilemma when his own impending death forces him to make provisions for a people, the Ocampa, he has cared for over many centuries and with whom he clearly has a godlike relationship. Subsequent episodes looked favorably upon the ancient Native American beliefs of Commander Chakotay, including the belief in animal guides, as evidenced by Captain Kathryn Janeway's enthusiastic embracing of such techniques and her pursuit of such a guide for herself and her crew. After a tantalizing start that included a brilliant exploration of questions about resurrection and life after death (see the episode "Emanations," aired March 1995), *Voyager* largely retreated from intense religious themes, whereas *Deep Space Nine* continued to elaborate upon them.

The differences among the series are best understood as the consequences of several factors. Roddenberry's well-documented views on religion played a major role in the representation of religion in the Original Series, *Next Generation*, and

the early films. Yet he was keenly sensitive to the religious pro-
clivities of the American audience, and he was not above pan-
dering so as not to offend viewers, sponsors, and the network.
The Original Series and *Next Generation* reflect not only the
views of Roddenberry and his many writers but also the complex and changing role of religion in American life. Thus, the
extrusion of deeply religious themes into *Deep Space Nine* can
be partly understood as a reflection of an increasing public
discourse regarding religion.

In America, terms like "religion," "religions," and "religious" are
used so frequently and ordinarily that few people would think
them vague or imprecise. Most of us think we know what we
mean when we call something a "religion" or identify some practices, beliefs, institutions, or persons as "religious." Yet many lan-
guages do not have closely corresponding terms, and some recent theorists of religion have suggested that religion is a
relatively modern concept invented by Western culture rather
than just a convenient label for a universal human phenomenon.
    Although we are well aware of the methodological difficul-
ties in using terms like "religion" and "religious," we have written this book with a specific audience in mind and intentionally use ordinary language to make our points. In this regard,
our approach is similar to that of the Star Trek writers, who
crafted TV scripts and screenplays that are sophisticated yet
use common language and imagery to depict religion.
    The religion they depict is usually the creation of those writ-
ers, including Gene Roddenberry. These are remarkably good
facsimiles of Terran religions, whether intentionally or not;
they can be parodies that function within a single episode or
film; they can also be a pastiche of actual religions that we

would never expect to find in a single coherent system. They may, at times, offer a transparent parallel to religions or religious conflicts of our own time. Viewed in this context, the religions of Star Trek say more about the writers than about anyone who might participate in them.

Regardless of the varied religious aspects depicted in Star Trek, there is no question as to the suspicion of organized, didactic forms of religion and the relatively liberal, humanistic leanings of the entire series. Despite the more serious treatment of religion in *Next Generation*, *Deep Space Nine*, and *Voyager*, Trek scrupulously avoids endorsing any religious claim in particular or religious sensibility in general, apparently preferring to keep its options open. The survival of Roddenberry's skepticism is, in the end, never at risk.

Insofar as Star Trek gives us imaginal religion (including, occasionally, imaginal rites), we are mostly interested in those imaginings and how they change over time—in representations of religion, that is. And because religion in Trek is never an accurate representation of Terran religion, we have decided to abstain from engaging in extensive debates about theories of religion and ritual. We do call attention to the ways in which Star Trek's representations of religion share and illustrate the same views as any number of theorists of religion. For the most part, however, we illuminate how Star Trek represents religion, considering more why it might do so in the ways that it does, and less on analyzing the religions as religions or rituals as rituals.

Part of what makes Star Trek so attractive for religion scholars is its diversity of opinions and perspectives. Because many writers, directors, actors, and others have played such an essential role in each chapter of the Star Trek canon, there is both richness and inconsistency. Indeed, it seems like you can't have one without the other. The fact that this is so often true of actual religions makes the issue familiar, if not altogether agreeable, to us as scholars. The fact that Star Trek is cumulative—that is, it constantly refers to itself and develops its canon by adding and deepening plot lines, characters, and worldview—is similarly familiar to us.

Although we gained some access to the intentions of Star Trek's creator, Gene Roddenberry, our reluctance to pursue the intentions of the writers was more theoretical and ideological. People's expressions of their own intentions are simply one more piece in a rich mosaic of analysis. Certainly, what authors say about their own writing should not be discounted, but practitioners offer wildly different explanations for why they practice some particular ritual or observance. There is no definitive explanation for why peoples undertake particular ceremonies and actions, and the accepted explanations change over time from community to community. Accordingly, we contend that some consistency in the representation of religion emerges in Star Trek despite the diversity of its authors. It is far from complete, pervasive, and total, but it nevertheless offers an intriguing coherence.[1]

Roddenberry once admitted that he pulled his punches when it came to the subject of religion. He felt it was not his place to vent his feelings on God and religion to the point that it became hurtful to people or their feelings. A story he tells of an episode he wrote for *Have Gun Will Travel*, a popular TV series in the 1960s, suggests that the occasional and seemingly inconsistent religious observance or idea in Star Trek was largely arbitrary and more of a sop to his audiences than anything else.

Once in a penitentiary where a pastor was trying to keep a fellow from being hung, I wrote that the pastor grabbed a hacksaw blade, was cut by it, and was bleeding. I had him make some comment about blood and salvation. It's not that I actually believed in blood and salvation being connected, but that was the way the audience believed (*Humanist* 1991:7).

Here we may have a viable explanation of everything from the positive retelling of the emergence of Christianity in "Bread and Circuses" to Kirk's remark to Apollo that humans find "the One [God]" quite adequate. Yet Roddenberry also conceded that in his vision of the future religious belief and practice does not so much disappear as retire to the private realm. It was pointed out to him that the basic outlook of the *Enterprise* crew seemed to be humanistic. He replied:

Oh, yes. They have their own beliefs, which are private to them, and they don't evangelize or go around discussing them with other people. I've always assumed that by this time [the twenty-fourth century] there is a belief that is common to people in Star Trek that yes, there is something out there. There is, perhaps, something that guides our lives but we don't know what it is and we don't know *if* it is (*Humanist* 1991:28).

This view of the future—in which religious beliefs persist as a private matter yet whose competing claims provoke no conflict—is perplexing. At the very least, it suggests a view of religion as personal and private. In modern America, where the rights and needs of individuals have acquired a privilege virtually unknown in other cultures, such an imagining of the future is perhaps understandable. Still, it flies in the face of much religion scholarship that recognizes the strong degree to which religion is almost always deeply implicated in social, communal, and public life. Shared rites and beliefs create and reflect an understanding of how the universe is, which makes social life possible: A society full of people with vastly differing, conflicting beliefs is one whose potential for dysfunction is enormous, something Roddenberry seems not to understand.

Although Roddenberry's views permeate Star Trek, the absence of religion—or at least any public, communal Terran religion in the third millenium—also fits well with Star Trek's generally optimistic, almost utopian view of the future, in which all the concerns addressed by religions—poverty, illness, social inequity, injustice, ecological crises—have been solved (obliterating or altering the traditional functions of much modern religious belief, if not practice). Roddenberry may not have been aware of this inconsistency.

But modern American politics makes it difficult to present a future in which one religious tradition emerges triumphant. Roddenberry related an interesting story regarding this very issue in the Original Series. The network, it seems, wanted a chaplain on the *Enterprise*. This struck him as absurd: "Presumably, each one of the worlds we were dealing with was very much like Earth in that several religions must have arisen over time. Contending religions. How could you have a chaplain if you've got that many people of different and alien beliefs on your ship?" (*Humanist* 1991:6).

Equally absurd to him was the time that writers and producers wanted to conduct a Christian funeral ceremony for a temporarily deceased Spock, the science officer. In Roddenberry's view, his writers had failed to understand that one wouldn't conduct a Christian burial for a Vulcan—or that Christian funerals were conducted in the first place given the diversity of traditions. Instead, Roddenberry envisioned the kinds of neutral, generic, civil ceremonies that we see occasionally for Star Trek funerals and weddings, including the real funeral of Spock in *Search for Spock*. Roddenberry, of course, failed to see that the private beliefs of future peoples would make such civil ceremonies insufficient, if not dangerously inadequate. Subsequent writers seem to understand this better.

After Roddenberry's death in 1991, the producers and writers began to offer richer and more complex representations of religious practices, beliefs, and worldviews, most extensively in the cosmic religious drama that *Deep Space Nine* became. Whereas Roddenberry and the Original Series writers envisioned the United Federation of Planets as largely devoid of religion—religion being an attribute of primitive, prescientific "others"—the writers and producers of *Deep Space Nine* and *Voyager* seem to kindle a kind of religious revival. In the twenty-fourth century of the latter two series, religion can still be the province of the "Other," but they have begun to encroach much more upon the "us" of Starfleet. Yet even the later shows never stray too far from Roddenberry's humanistic faith in human free will and the salvific nature of dispassionate scientific inquiry.

This change over the thirty years of Star Trek corresponds to the changing place of religion in American public discourse and to the resurgence of religion in America. As the twenty-third century reflects the 1960s, the twenty-fourth century reflects the 1980s and 1990s. Nevertheless, Star Trek is not a simple mirror of debates about religion in America: It is still a TV show that reflects the skepticism and profound humanism of its creator as well as the practical constraints of consumer television. Those constraints meant that Star Trek could not represent any modern religion as triumphant, and presenting them all as surviving into the twenty-fourth century presented a problem in and of itself. Given the recent divisiveness associated with religious differences in the world, how could the writers of Star Trek present the Federation as united and above such petty divisiveness yet imagine that the religious traditions that undergird our contemporary cultural and political conflicts still exist? Then there is the real problem of setting the cosmos of the twenty-fourth century, with its multiplicity of beings and cultures, within the limited framework of current religions, a cosmos that seems to contradict many tenets of those same traditions. Such a task is not inherently impossible, of course. But one can easily understand why Star Trek's writers, Roddenberry included, would rather avoid the whole messy issue.

In the twenty-fourth century, then, Terrans may be spiritual, but they are certainly not adherents of twenty-fourth-century versions of twentieth-century religions. If, as Roddenberry claimed, Terrans have their own "indigenous" religious lives, neither he nor his successors show them to us. (*Voyager's* Chakotay is the sole possible exception here; and even he is portrayed more in an imprecise fashion as "spiritual." This spirituality is highly individual, rather than communal, and Chakotay lacks any religious community.) What we do see in *Deep Space Nine* and, to a lesser extent, in *Voyager* are Terrans open to the possibility of some vague and ill-defined personal "spirituality" yet skeptical about the claims of any life-form or culture on questions of religion in Terran traditions—the nature and existence of divinity, the nature and existence of evil, life after death, the creation of the cosmos, and even how to live a righteous life.

In this book, we wish to consider precisely these kinds of questions.

Is There God in the Universe?

ROSS S. KRAEMER

Most mythology has its basis in fact.
—James T. Kirk, "Who Mourns for Adonais?"

If the United Federation of Planets decided to undertake a mission to answer the primary question posed in this chapter—Is there God?—there would be any number of potential and aspiring deities in the Star Trek universe. Many, of course, would quickly be disqualified as pretenders. The real problem would be in determining what it would take to merit the label "God" (or god). Gene Roddenberry and Star Trek's many writers would be of little help on this point. As with Terran theologians over many centuries, Star Trek's creators seem to have had difficulty formulating an adequate definition, for the criteria for true divinity are never made explicit in the series.

Yet the catalog of patently false gods covers the entire series, from the inanimate Vaal and the ancient Greek gods from the Original Series, to the charlatan Ardra in *Next Generation*, to the compassionate if misguided Caretaker of *Voyager*. Interestingly, however, throughout Star Trek the "reality" of candidates for divinity is rarely, if ever, in doubt (although the long-dead ancient Klingon gods might prove an intriguing exception). Rather, it is always their identity that is at stake, in contradiction to Terran gods, whose very existence is continually the subject of heated controversy.

Gods Who Aren't

Tailor-made for a religious studies class, "The Apple," an episode from the second season of the Original Series, depicts a primitive people bound in an unhealthy symbiotic relationship with an ancient mechanical power source they unquestioningly accept as a god. Consistent with the biblical allusion of the title, the episode is full of additional transparent references to the Hebrew Bible. The powerful god-machine is called Vaal, an obvious reference to the Canaanite deity Ba'al so often vilified in the Hebrew Bible. The physical representation of Vaal, a vast, reptilian, stone face with glowing eyes and a fiery furnace for a mouth seems to have come straight from the depiction of idols who required human sacrifices (such as the god Molech) envisioned in Hollywood epic films.

The people of Vaal, as they call themselves, live in a paradisiacal environment similar to that of Genesis 2:4–3:24, characterized by idyllic conditions absent in ordinary human life.
The planet possesses an ideal climate, lush tropical vegetation,
and an atmosphere that apparently screens out harmful radiation. Its people are easily recognizable as "primitive": They live
in modest thatched huts, wear simple white clothing, decorate
their faces with strange painted markings, and adorn their
bodies with flowers (perhaps a transparent allusion to 1960s
flower children). If we may judge by the food they leave for
the crew, they eat a simple, vegetarian diet (like Adam and
Eve, apparent vegans while in the Garden of Eden). They display no signs of advanced civilization or technology. Violence
is clearly unknown to them, as is sexual behavior, and they
have no children. Their bodies are not aging. In fact, they resemble angels in ancient Jewish and Christian traditions in numerous ways: They are asexual, ageless, perhaps immortal, apparently ignorant of death; they wear white, live peacefully,
and their only real purpose appears to be to serve Vaal. They
do, however, differ in at least one crucial way—there are both
male and female people of Vaal, whereas ancient Jewish and
Christian accounts of angels contain no references to female
angels. On their planet, as in the biblical Eden, Paradise is
characterized by the abundant presence of uncultivated food
and the absence of sexuality, children, aging, illness, and
death.

These inhabitants of Gamma Trianguli VI believe that Vaal is
sentient and powerful, although dependent on their ministra-
tions. Vaal exhibits some of the characteristics of living beings:
He hungers and must be fed; at times he sleeps. The inhabitants attribute to him powers that Terrans often associate with
divinity: He causes the rain to fall and the sun to shine, and all

good things come from him. One of the first manifestations of
Vaal that we see is in a massive and threatening cloud formation that quickly becomes a powerful lightning storm, alluding in all likelihood to the characterization of the Canaanite
Ba'al (and his nemesis, the God of Israel) as a storm god. Vaal's
relationship with his people is mediated through a man
named Akuta, who describes himself as the "eyes and voice" of
Vaal. Only Akuta can speak to Vaal, and Vaal speaks only to
him. Akuta has antennae implanted behind his ears that he
says Vaal gave to him in the "dim time," so that the people of
Vaal could serve and obey him. Of course, Vaal is imagined to
be male.

From the perspective of the *Enterprise* crew, however, Vaal is
quite different. A force-field of some sort prevents the crew
from getting close to Vaal, but Mr. Spock is quickly able to determine that Vaal is artificial, of ancient workmanship, and
generates great power. The crew sees Vaal as nothing but an
access point for the unseen power source.

The discovery of a seeming paradise on Gamma Trianguli
VI, and of the unquestioning faith of its inhabitants in the divinity of Vaal and his crucial role in their well-being, poses serious dilemmas for the *Enterprise* crew. Differing views are put
into the mouths of the Vulcan Spock and the chief medical officer, Doctor Leonard "Bones" McCoy. McCoy expresses horror
at the dependence of the planet's inhabitants on this false deity,
whom they must regularly feed energy-bearing rocks, and
who deters them from the ordinary pleasures of life, work,
sexuality, and child-rearing—or what McCoy calls "the normal
course of social evolution." "This isn't life," he contends, "it's
stagnation." Spock, in contrast, challenges McCoy's views of
normal evolution and offers a relativist position: The inhabitants are happy and well cared for, ignorant of the alternatives.

Who are the crew of the *Enterprise* to intervene?

When Vaal becomes a threat to the survival of *Enterprise*, the debate becomes more than academic. Unless the ship engineer, Scotty, and his staff can find a solution to the power losses on the *Enterprise* obviously caused by Vaal, it will be dragged down to the planet's surface. In the meantime, two of Vaal's people, a male and female, observe Lieutenant Pavel Chekov and a female crew member kissing passionately. Concluding that such behavior appears to be pleasant, they try it themselves, only to be discovered and chastised by Akuta.

Vaal then communicates to Akuta that the strangers are dangerous enemies who must be destroyed, and he orders them killed. But killing and death are unknown to the inhabitants: When they ask Akuta what "killing" is, he tells them it is just something "to do" to the strangers. Akuta must show them what Vaal has in mind using a coconutlike fruit to demonstrate how to bash the *Enterprise* crew over the head.

Unaware that the inhabitants are now training to kill, the crew again debates their own actions. McCoy and Captain Kirk are horrified by the life the inhabitants lead, consisting as it does solely of the care and feeding of themselves and Vaal, devoid of significant work, sexuality, and struggle. Spock takes the position that even though these people (the show repeatedly calls them "humanoid") aren't ideal, they are "viable," and so he is opposed to altering their way of life. But now Kirk takes a stance: He is deeply offended that the inhabitants of the planet exist just to serve a machine, and he intentionally chooses to violate the Federation's Prime Directive (a directive of noninterference), which prohibits the *Enterprise* from interfering in the normal development of another society.

Shortly, the inhabitants unsuccessfully attack the crew, intensifying Kirk's need to solve his twin dilemma of saving the

Enterprise and the inhabitants from Vaal. Spock interprets their learning to kill cynically, as the first step on the (dubious) road to becoming human. Again, like his biblical counterparts, Vaal appears in the form of storm clouds and attacks Spock.

Blaming himself for the harm done to his crew, Kirk decides to prevent the people from feeding Vaal—holding them captive inside a hut. Vaal begins to lose power, enabling a phaser attack from the desperate *Enterprise* to weaken and destroy it. Once Vaal is dead, Kirk instructs his crew to "let those people go" in yet another transparent biblical allusion to Moses, if not to God. This offhand fusion of the biblical creation narrative with the Exodus story is not as random as it might seem at first; in Jewish tradition, the two events are repeatedly linked in observance and retellings.

Faced with the realization that Vaal is gone, the people are hardly overjoyed. When they point out that Vaal cared for them, Kirk replies, "Now you'll have to care for yourselves." McCoy observes that these people have now been set on the "normal course of social evolution." In a closing scene, Kirk confidently assures the smiling people of Vaal that they will love freedom, sexual love, children, responsibility, and independence.

In this episode, authentic existence requires humans to take full responsibility for themselves. It seems to suggest, although not explicitly, that authentic existence also requires recognition of the falseness of "god." Interestingly we learn little about Vaal beyond the fact that it is ancient and artificial. We know nothing about what Vaal is, who created Vaal, for what purposes, and how Vaal actually works, and we don't need to: This is a false god, which is all that matters. The crux of the show is the destruction of Vaal and the demonstration of his false nature.

In the closing scene, Spock and McCoy reprise their debate about whether they have done the right thing. Countering Mc-Coy's conviction that they have, Spock turns to Kirk and asks whether he is familiar with the "biblical story of Genesis." When Kirk says, "Of course," Spock points out that "we have given the people of Vaal the apple, the knowledge of good and evil, if you will, as a result of which they, too, have been driven out of paradise." In a scene intended to be humorous, Kirk asks whether he's being cast in the role of Satan, or whether anyone else on the ship looks remotely like Satan. The camera focuses on Spock's famously pointed ears, but the light-hearted music cues us that this is not to be taken seriously.

Genesis here is relegated to ancient Earth myth, well-known, perhaps, to educated persons Terran and otherwise but no longer revered, let alone believed, by any of the crew and, by implication, anyone in the Federation. (The actual text of Genesis, however, appears not so well known, as neither "apple" nor "Satan" actually appears in the Hebrew text or any careful modern translation; what we see in this vignette may illustrate the tenacity of popular forms of tradition.) *Star Trek V: The Final Frontier*, will give us only a slightly different take on the preservation of such myths.

The "myth" of the expulsion from Eden in Genesis is not merely relegated to the past in "The Apple"; it is also critiqued in the very way in which it is recast. Many commentators on the biblical Garden narrative have recognized that the departure from Eden narrates a transition from idyllic conditions to those of ordinary human existence. In Paradise there may be no work, no sexuality, no children, no culture, and no death; in the real world humans work for their food, make love, have children, invent things, kill, and die. "The Apple" narrates a similar tale, set appropriately on a seemingly paradisiacal planet. As we have seen, life on Gamma Trianguli VI is initially characterized by these same paradisiacal circumstances: absence of work, sexuality, children, culture, illness, and death. At the show's conclusion, the people of Vaal will experience all these things.

There are, however, some important differences. In Genesis, the serpent tempts Eve and Adam into disobedience of God; in "The Apple" Chekov and his female companion indirectly (but perhaps deliberately) tempt two inhabitants. But they are never directly offered the same choice as Eve, when the serpent urges her to eat of the forbidden fruit of the Tree of Knowledge of good and evil. Instead, Kirk, as captain, makes a series of decisions that force the innocent inhabitants out of paradise and into what McCoy calls "the normal course of social evolution."

Furthermore, in Genesis the departure from Eden is seen as punishment for disobedience (note, however, that the word "sin," like "apple" and "Satan," does not occur in the biblical text but is instead the result of subsequent interpretations), contributing to its understanding as negative, as a "fall" (yet another term absent from the biblical text). In the Original Series, the transition from Paradise is viewed much more positively and is not the result of intentional action—let alone deliberate defiance—on the part of the inhabitants. Although the scenarios are similar, the valuations are largely reversed.

Finally, in Genesis God's relationship with Adam and Eve, and with their descendants, continues, if altered by the disobedience of the first couple. In "The Apple," the departure from Paradise is dependent upon a severing of the ties between the people and Vaal. Since in fact Vaal is not God at all but simply a machine whose creators are unknown and apparently long gone, the transition into "normal social evolution" requires the destruction, or at least the deactivation, of Vaal and its power over these people. It seems, then, that in this episode authentic human existence requires the death of God.

Several other shows were devoted not only to demonstrating the falsehood and dangers of beliefs like those initially held by the people of Vaal but also to offering explanations for why Terrans might initially themselves have held such beliefs but subsequently abandoned them. This was the central theme of the 1967 episode "Who Mourns for Adonais?" This episode revealed the ancient Greek gods to be extraterrestrial beings who departed Earth when human beings ceased to worship them.

The episode's title alludes to a line from a poem by Percy Bysshe Shelley entitled "Adonais: An Elegy on the Death of John Keats," but it is also clearly draws on ancient Mediterranean rites of mourning for the Syrian god Adonis. In some ancient myths, Adonis was the beautiful young lover of the Syrian goddess, in others of the Greek Aphrodite, and in still others of Persephone, the daughter of Demeter. After dying a tragic accidental death, Adonis was mourned by his divine lover, as well as by human women in annual festivals celebrated in many cities, according to several ancient authors. The Star Trek Apollo's transformation of the ship's anthropologist, Caroline, into a goddess figure (he replaces her Starfleet uniform with a Grecian-style dress and elaborate hairstyle reminiscent of ancient goddess statues and paintings), and her subsequent grief upon his death, can easily be understood as additional allusions to these ancient traditions. Many American viewers are unlikely to have caught the references, although those schooled in Greek mythology (as a considerable number of Star Trek's early audiences may have been) would have been somewhat more likely to catch on.

Both "The Apple" and "Who Mourns for Adonais?" demonstrate a prevailing theme in Star Trek that religious beliefs have their basis in erroneous interpretation of empirical experiences. In "The Apple," a primitive and ignorant people mistakes a powerful machine for a divine creator and protector, whereas in "Who Mourns for Adonais?" the ancient Greeks themselves mistook powerful extraterrestrial beings for gods. Once again, it is the physician McCoy who makes the observation that to the ancient (and relatively ignorant) Greeks these powerful galactic visitors would have seemed like gods. Fortunately for the Starship *Enterprise*, Kirk and his companions are not so easily misled on either count: They persist in their efforts to identify a technological basis for the power of the "deity," inevitably resulting in the successful neutralization of that power.

The take on worship of divine pretenders in "Who Mourns for Adonais?" is somewhat more sympathetic than that of "The Apple," perhaps because, as McCoy observes, to "simple shepherds" of ancient Greece beings like Apollo "could have been taken for gods" and couldn't have been taken for anything else given their extraordinary powers (including apparent immortality). Apollo's offer of an ordered paradisiacal life on Earth in exchange for loyalty, tribute, and worship seems like a bargain many would once have found appealing.

Yet in a key scene in "Who Mourns for Adonais?" Captain Kirk asserts that such a relationship is no longer viable. Defiantly responding to Apollo's demands for obedience and worship, Kirk retorts: "We've come a long way in 5,000 years. Mankind has no need for gods. . . . We've outgrown you. You ask for something we can no longer give." The fact that Apollo has the power to make Kirk and the *Enterprise* suffer for this response in no way persuades them that Apollo deserves anything other than resistance. Ultimately, Apollo himself concedes that the other gods were right: The time is past and there is no longer room for gods.

Astute Star Trek fans may realize that we've left out one crucial line of Kirk's response to Apollo. After he tells Apollo that mankind "has no need for gods," the apparently irreligious Kirk claims "we find the one quite adequate." As our introductory discussion of Roddenberry's tactics for dealing with the religious sensibilities of his audiences suggests, such a line seems more likely to be one of the creator's throwaway lines designed to mollify American viewers than any serious indication of Kirk's offended or outraged monotheist beliefs. Kirk might even be understood to suggest that one god is more than enough to handle.

The *Next Generation* series reprises these themes in somewhat more sophisticated dress. In the cleverly constructed plot of "Who Watches the Watchers?" inhabitants of Mintaka III erroneously come to believe that the *Enterprise's* captain is himself a divine being whom they call "the Picard." The Federation has set up an observation station on the planet to keep tabs on the inhabitants, who resemble Romulans and Vulcans and whose evolution, we are told, closely parallels that of the Vulcans. Although their technology is still quite limited (they hunt with bows and arrows), they are rational, intelligent, and peaceful.

As the episode begins, the observation station (concealed on a mountainside) experiences a power failure that renders its cloaking features ineffectual, and a scientist named Palmer is thrown out the window and injured. At the same time, two Mintakans, a young woman named Oji and her father, Liko, are on their way up the mountain. Oji is about to take an official reading of the sundial—apparently taking over the role of her recently deceased mother—when they see flashes of light coming from the station.

Liko climbs up to investigate and he, too, is wounded by a power surge while peering into the window. Since he has already seen members of the *Enterprise* away team beamed down to aid the scientists, the chief medical officer, Doctor Beverly Crusher, decides to beam him up to sick bay. Picard is initially annoyed at this violation of the Prime Directive and instructs Doctor Crusher to try a dicey procedure to wipe out Liko's short-term memory before returning him, healed, to the planet's surface. The scene in which Liko watches Picard in a cloudlike haze foreshadows the failure of the procedure and the deification of the captain.

Returned home alive and well, Liko tells his overjoyed daughter that he has encountered a divine being known in ancient Mintakan traditions as the Overseer, a being who has brought him back to life.

> Oji: I was sure you were dead.
> Liko: I think I was, but I was brought back to life. I awoke in an incredible place and my wounds were gone. I had been healed.
> Oji: How is that possible?
> Liko [hesitating]: Long ago, our people believed in beings with great powers, and those beings made the rains come. They told the sun when to rise, they caused all life to be born, to grow, to die. . . .
> Oji: But those are just tales, Father, old superstitions. . . .
> Liko: But perhaps the beliefs of our ancestors are true—nothing else can explain what's happened.

Although there is, of course, a very different explanation for what happened to Liko, a subsequent scene plays with the idea that relatively primitive people like the Mintakans could only explain Liko's experience by recourse to divine beings. First Officer William Riker and the ship's counselor, Deanna Troi, disguised as Mintakans, happen upon Liko sharing his tale with others:

> Liko [to an older male Mintakan]: You know the old legends well—do they not speak of beings like I've seen?
> Older Mintakan: There are stories of the Overseer who could appear at will, had supreme powers, could heal the dead.

When Liko replies that he believes he has seen the Overseer, who is called the Picard, Riker and Troi realize they have a serious problem on their hands. The apparent ability of Picard and his companions to heal the sick, raise the dead, and appear and disappear at will is explicable only as the work of a god: The idea that these powers are nothing more than mundane twenty-fourth-century Federation technology is incomprehensible. The accidental exposure of the observation station has triggered the recurrence of ancient Mintakan beliefs in supernatural beings.

The realization that this is a bad thing that needs to be corrected becomes clear in a central scene between Picard and the observation station's Doctor Barron. The Mintakans have, in the interim, found the wounded Palmer and have identified him as a servant of the Picard. Because they came upon him in a cave, they surmise that he had disobeyed the Picard and was hiding from his wrath. They argue that by keeping Palmer safe they will please the Overseer (Picard), who has the ability to bring gentle winters and even resurrect the dead. Doctor

Barron demands that Picard beam up the injured Palmer, but Picard is reluctant to do so because the use of beaming technology will further fuel the Mintakans' false beliefs in him.

When Riker successfully escapes with Palmer and beams back to the *Enterprise*, the Mintakans seize Deanna Troi. Liko advocates punishing Troi to let the Picard know that Troi and Riker helped in freeing Palmer. Now Doctor Barron pressures Picard to use the Mintakans' beliefs to free Troi. "The Mintakans wish to please the Overseer but they can only guess what he wants. They need a sign." Picard is horrified at Barron's suggestion that Picard masquerade as a god to provide what the doctor calls "guidelines" for what the Picard expects:

> Picard: I cannot, I will not, impose a set of commandments on these people.
> Doctor Barron: Like it or not, we have rekindled the Mintakans' belief in the Overseer.
> Riker: Are you saying this belief will develop into a religion?
> Doctor Barron: It's inevitable. And without guidance, that religion will degenerate into inquisitions, holy wars, chaos.
> Picard [after several seconds of silence]: Horrifying. [More silence, while Picard paces.] Millennia ago, they abandoned their belief in the supernatural—now you are asking me to sabotage that achievement—to send them back into the dark ages of superstition and ignorance and fear? NO!!!

Picard concludes he will have to find another way.

As in "The Apple," the plot of "Who Watches the Watchers?" denies the *Enterprise* the ability to escape from the dilemma simply by speeding away into space. In "The Apple," Vaal himself held the *Enterprise* captive; in "Who Watches the Watchers?" the crisis is a more complex moral dilemma for Picard:

encouraging the dangerous false beliefs of the Mintakans in order to save counselor Troi. Picard concludes that his only option is to persuade the Mintakans that he is, in fact, not divine.

Beaming their rational, judicious, and scientifically minded leader, a woman named Nuria, up to the *Enterprise*, Picard tries to persuade her that his powers are simply those of an advanced technological knowledge that her people, too, will one day attain. Convinced that he has succeeded, Picard is temporarily stymied when Nuria implores him to resurrect six Mintakans who recently died in floods. She refuses to believe that such a deed is beyond his powers; he has, after all, done the same thing for Liko. Only when she witnesses the death of Mary Warren, the third scientist on the observation station, does she recognize that Picard has been telling her the truth.

Meanwhile, back on the planet, things have deteriorated. When Nuria fails to reappear and a storm rages on the surface (the storm-god motif again), Liko becomes convinced that what the Picard truly desires is the death of Troi. In a scene that encapsulates Western theological debates, Troi points out that Liko does not truly know what the Picard wants—he is only guessing, and the consequences of his guessing wrong could be disastrous:

> Troi [relatively calm as Liko aims an arrow at her]: Liko, you
>   don't want to kill me.
> Liko: I must do as the Picard wishes.
> Troi: Are you sure you know what he wants? That's the problem
>   with believing in a supernatural being—trying to determine
>   what he wants.
> Liko: We must do *something*.
> Oji: But what if it's the wrong thing, father?

In seeming despair, Liko invokes the Picard's guidance. "Is it your wish that this woman should die? Answer us, speak!" At this moment Picard and Nuria appear and Picard does speak, admonishing Liko that he is not a god. Nuria affirms Picard's words, but Liko responds with skepticism in a scene that parodies, perhaps, the public's response to contemporary humans who claim to have been transported to spaceships and shown (or subjected to) alien technology. The scene also evokes religious officials' responses to scientists whose work conflicts with received truths, such as the Roman Catholic Church's condemnation of Galileo for demonstrating that the Earth revolves around the sun.

Now the death of Liko's wife plays a pivotal role in the plot. Still persuaded that Picard has the power of life and death, Liko replays the earlier scene with Nuria and Picard, imploring the captain to bring back his wife. Despite Picard's protestations that he cannot do so, Liko insists that he can, then draws his bow to shoot Picard in order to prove the latter's imperviousness to death. Only when Picard is wounded and bleeding does Liko concede that Picard is not, in fact, divine but merely a mortal of another species. After the typical farewells from the crew, the *Enterprise* goes on its way, captain and crew greatly relieved that they have not restored dangerous beliefs in gods and that their violation of the Prime Directive has caused no irreparable harm.

Although far more sophisticated in plot, dialogue, and set than "The Apple," *Next Generation*'s "Who Watches the Watchers?" takes essentially the same stance on the same issues. Belief in capricious divine beings, seemingly justified however it may be in actual experience, deters natural and beneficial "human" progress. Left to their own devices, intelligent humanoid life-forms will eventually renounce such superstitions in favor of rational scientific understandings of the universe. Belief in such beings leads to communal strife and conflict and the willingness to commit barbarous acts. In "The Apple," the previously peaceful people of Gamma Trianguli VI, when commanded by Vaal, prepare to murder the crew of the *Enterprise* by bashing them over the head with rocks, whereas in "Who Watches the Watchers?" the inability to discern the will of the Picard prompts frightened people to undertake the execution of innocent *Enterprise* crew members. At the very least, evolutionary progress requires the abandonment of false beliefs in false gods, with no indication that there are any true gods in whom it would be better to believe.

Still, "Who Watches the Watchers?" contributes to the idea that the "god" in whom it would be better not to believe is still to be construed as all-powerful and immortal. Picard's attempts to dissuade the Mintakans of his divinity involve demonstrating his inability to restore the dead to life, the reality of his own mortality, and the source of his powers in scientifically explicable technology and processes.

A somewhat more lighthearted episode, "Devil's Due" (*Next Generation*, February 1991) offered us yet another false deity— with a twist. In a plot that borrowed heavily and obviously from the story of Faust, the war-weary people of Ventax II had made a dangerous bargain with a deity named Ardra. In exchange for a thousand years of peace and prosperity, they had sold their descendants into perpetual economic and personal slavery to Ardra. When the episode begins, the thousand years has just come to an end, and the Ventaxians are in a state of high anxiety anticipating the return of Ardra—and the imminent payment of the bargain made by their ancestors. Although Picard and his companions are skeptical of this ancient Ventaxian legend, they are quickly drawn into the dilemma through the standard plot devices. A beautiful and seemingly powerful being who claims to be Ardra holds the Enterprise hostage and compels Data to adjudicate the Ventaxian legal dispute over the ancient contract.

The clever and persistent Enterprise crew ultimately locates and exposes the power sources of the pretender, as in "The Apple" and "Who Mourns for Adonais?" Meanwhile, the audience is treated to scenes of the beautiful Ardra, who is unsuccessfully seducing the high-minded, resistant, and virtuous Captain Picard. This seemingly secondary aspect of the plot simultaneously draws on and partially reverses the underlying plot of Faust. In that story, the uncontrolled desires of Faust for the beautiful Marguerite prompt his bargain with the devil and cause him to sell his soul; in the "Devil's Due" episode, Picard's self-control allows him to resist the devil and save the Enterprise and the Ventaxians. Although the devil is a male being in Faust and is female in "Devil's Due," both stories draw on the same gendered stereotypes: Beautiful women pose a mortal threat to the male protagonist.

Unlike Apollo—who appears to have believed his own claims to divinity in "Who Mourns for Adonais?"—Ardra in "Devil's Due" turns out to be nothing more than a high-tech alien trickster who impersonates the goddess of Ventaxian tradition for personal gain. The question of whether there was ever a real "Ardra" is left unanswered, as is any consideration of whether the character should be considered divine, demonic, or both. (In Chapter 2, we return to the question of whether Ardra sheds light on the question of evil.)

The inaugural episode of Star Trek: Voyager, the last of the TV series, provides viewers with yet another candidate for divinity. In "Caretaker" a powerful being is faced with an extraordinary dilemma when his own impending death forces him to make provisions for a people, the Ocampa, he has cared for over many centuries and with whom he clearly has a godlike relationship. Many years ago, the surface of the fifth planet of their star became too hot for the Ocampa to inhabit, and the Caretaker designed and built underground cities, supplying water and food-production units for the Ocampa; they have resided there ever since. Another species—a people known as the Kazon—continues to inhabit the surface of the planet, although they are desperate for water and would plunder the Ocampa if they could get to them.

The Caretaker never communicates directly with the Ocampa, forcing them (like Liko in "Who Watches the Watchers?") to try to discern his will from indirect evidence. Periodically, the Caretaker sends the Ocampa diseased persons whom they try to care for as best they can, without knowing why he has sent them. *Voyager* becomes embroiled in this situation when the Caretaker seizes both it and a rebel Maquis ship from a vast distance, capturing a crew member from each—Harry Kim from *Voyager* and B'Elanna Torres from the Maquis. Both Harry and B'Elanna end up seriously ill and in the care of the Ocampa.

The Ocampa relationship with the unseen Caretaker prompts serious debate among the subterranean people. Although many consider the Caretaker to be a benevolent protector, others (like the soon-to-be *Voyager* crew member Kes) insist that the Ocampa have lost their cognitive abilities and become unhealthily dependent on the Caretaker. Kes and an Ocampa named Toskit debate whether they should submit to the uncertain will of the Caretaker or seek their own path, returning to the surface of the planet to take their chances.

Although their limited knowledge causes the Ocampa to view their lives and relationship with the Caretaker in a manner that seems calculated to evoke Western religious tradition, the *Voyager* crew enjoys a different vantage point. The Vulcan officer, Tuvok, reasons that the Caretaker has given the Ocampa extra energy and sealed the conduits to the subterranean cities to prevent the Caissons from stealing the Ocampa water supplies because he (i.e., the Caretaker) is dying. Moreover, *Voyager's* crew discerns that it was the Caretaker himself who destroyed the atmosphere of the planet and created its ecological crisis, which is why he has cared for the Ocampa ever since. Realizing that he is dying, and lacking any offspring, the Caretaker has been searching unsuccessfully for a compatible biomolecular pattern among passing aliens, hoping to generate a replacement who will continue to care for the Ocampa.

As with the other episodes we have considered, the fate of the Federation starship becomes inextricably intertwined with that of the Ocampa. The Caretaker intends to destroy a power array to keep the Caissons from harming the Ocampa to harness the array. Yet this same installation enabled the Caretaker to bring *Voyager* from the Alpha Quadrant to the Delta Quadrant, and it is the crew's only hope of returning home in a reasonable time. The crew is thus presented with a moral dilemma: rescuing themselves and harming the Ocampa, or saving the Ocampa and stranding themselves in the Delta Quadrant.

Captain Kathryn Janeway implores the Caretaker to consider other options. Their dialogue echoes the themes of episodes from the Original Series and *Next Generation*:

> Janeway: Did you ever consider allowing the Ocampa to take care of themselves?
> The Caretaker: They're children.

Janeway: Children have to grow up—evolve—take care of themselves.

Yet before Janeway can persuade the Caretaker, a Caisson ship takes matters into its own hands, destroying the array. Abandoning his temporary form as an elderly Caucasian human male, the Caretaker reverts to some amorphous state and dies. The Ocampa are left vulnerable to the Caisson, and *Voyager* and the Maquis ship are stranded in the Delta Quadrant, far from home.

Foreshadowing the sophisticated treatment of religion in *Voyager* as a whole, the inaugural two-part episode offered a much subtler take on the existence of deities in the universe, as well as the problematic relationships between powerful beings taken for deities by less powerful and less knowledgeable beings. The plot of "Caretaker" bears some striking resemblances to ancient Western myths of the human condition that are often labeled "gnostic" (from the Greek *gnosis*, or "knowledge"—in this case knowledge of the true nature of the world and of the human condition). In many versions of these myths, humans have lost the knowledge of their true identity as divine sparks of light that have become weighed down in material bodies. Failing to know who they really are, they have come to worship a deity who they believe has created the material world, but who is himself misguided in his understanding of his true self. In some versions of these myths, this creator-deity has a female counterpart, with whom he has created this imperfect world. Ultimately, the true deity, from whom the divine sparks of light all emanate, sends a redeemer or savior down to the material realm to reveal their true identities to the fallen sparks and to show them how to escape from their inauthentic embodied existence and return to the heavenly realms from which they originally came. Many scholars of early Christianity have observed that the New Testament Gospel of John has many features of this narrative.

Although "Caretaker" is not a simplistic refashioning of an ancient gnostic myth, the similarities are significant. The Ocampa, or at least most Ocampa, have lost the knowledge of who they were before they came to live in relative darkness below the surface of the planet. They no longer know that in days past they were a competent, autonomous civilization, and they cannot imagine themselves as anything other than the childlike dependents of the Caretaker. Failing to discern the Caretaker's true identity and nature, the Ocampa revere him as a distant and powerful deity responsible for their well-being, with whom they cannot communicate directly, and whose will is inscrutable. The occasional Ocampa who escapes to the surface might challenge these beliefs and consider the possibility that the Ocampa once cared for themselves—and could learn to do so again—but such views are considered heretical and dangerous. Only when knowledgeable and powerful aliens intervene do the Ocampa gain a truer understanding of what they once were, what they have become, and what they might yet accomplish.

The missing elements vis-à-vis ancient gnostic narratives are, of course, any references to that true deity, or to the intervening aliens as themselves the emanations or agents of such a god. Instead, as we might well expect, knowledge of their true identity, and their ultimate potential, comes to the Ocampa by way of intelligent beings who are different only in their depth of knowledge and their abilities. The outsiders' greater knowledge allows the Ocampa to recognize the true nature of the Caretaker, as well as the inauthenticity of their prior dependent relationship with him, but it does not reveal the existence of a truer deity who had been concealed from the Caretaker as well.

This distinction is important. The absence of claims about a greater deity brings the ultimate message of this episode into closer conformity with earlier Star Trek episodes about false gods. In "Caretaker," as in all the episodes we have considered so far, beliefs in and relationships with powerful protective beings who demand infantile dependency and worship in return are inevitably bad for the worshipers. In "The Apple," Vaal's protection of the inhabitants of Gamma Trianguli VI deprives them of the fundamental joys of self-determination, freedom, sexual love, and children. Evolving Terrans renounce their need for the ancient gods since they became increasingly knowledgeable about the world and themselves. In "Who Watches the Watchers?" the people of Mintaka III abandon their ancient superstitious beliefs in gods as they become more knowledgeable and rational, and they come perilously close to backsliding when they mistake Picard for a god. In "Devil's Due" the Ventaxians actually bring about the peace and prosperity of the past thousand years on their own initiative, without the help of any divine being. They, too, run the risk of endangering their own advances when they almost accept the trickster alien for the ancient Ardra.

The implicit message of all these episodes, then, is not merely that the universe is full of divine pretenders. In some cases, after all, some do not so much claim their own divinity as have divinity falsely thrust upon them (like Picard in "Who Watches the Watchers"). Rather, succumbing to such claims or such beliefs is dangerous to the health, well-being, and autonomy of those who do.

The Falsest God of Them All: *Star Trek V*

Many televised Star Trek episodes have done nothing more than disqualify a particular candidate for divine status. But one film, directed by William Shatner under Roddenberry's aegis, intentionally confronted and explored theological questions, including the existence of God. In *Star Trek V: The Final Frontier*, the new and not altogether functional *Enterprise* is commandeered by a renegade Vulcan visionary named Sybok (who turns out to be Spock's half-brother) for a journey to encounter God. The actual journey to, and encounter with, the divine occupies only the last portion of the film.

Having journeyed to the center of the galaxy and passed safely through a region called the Great Barrier, where no ship had gone before, the *Enterprise* enters orbit around a legendary planet, called Sha Ka Ree by the Vulcans. Landing in a shuttle, Kirk, Spock, McCoy, and Sybok initially find nothing other than an empty landscape devoid of habitation. Soon, however, the skies darken and huge, monolithic stones erupt from the ground, curving in at the top to form a kind of sacred space evocative of Stonehenge. In the center of the space, lights begin to play, a wind roars, and a huge flame erupts upward. A deep voice then intones slowly, "Brave souls, welcome."

> McCoy: is this the voice of God?
> Voice: One voice, many faces.

Immediately we see various images of faces, ending with an old man with white hair and beard. "God" tells them they are the first to breach the Great Barrier and asks how they accomplished this feat. When Sybok tells him that they have come in a starship, God asks if the starship could carry his wisdom to the rest of creation. Sybok doesn't seem to notice the obvious theological dilemma—God, presumably all-powerful and all-knowing, by definition, has immediately displayed his ignorance. Kirk, however, picks up on this immediately.

> Kirk: Excuse me—I'd just like to ask a question. What does God need with a starship?

Voice: Bring the ship closer. . . .

Kirk: I said, what does God need with a starship?

Doctor McCoy: Jim, what are you doing?

Kirk: I'm asking a question.

Voice: Who is this creature?

Kirk: Who am I? Don't you know? Aren't you God?

Sybok: [Pointing to Kirk] He has his doubts. . . .

Voice: You doubt me?

Kirk: I seek proof.

Bones: Jim, you don't ask the Almighty for his ID.

Voice: Then here is the proof you seek. [He zaps Kirk with bolts of lightning shooting out from his eyes.]

Kirk [Recovering, on the ground] Why is God angry?

Sybok: Why, why have you done this to my friend?

Voice: He doubts me. . . .

Spock: You've not answered his question. What does God need with a starship? [He, too, gets zapped by lightning.]

This scene evokes doubt from Sybok as well. When he confronts God, pointing out that the god of Sha Ka Ree would not do this, God responds that "Sha Ka Ree [is] a vision *you* have created." Now we learn that the being has been imprisoned here for an eternity (although we never learn by whom or why). After Spock points out that this isn't the god of Sha Ka Ree or any place else, the being assumes the form of Sybok and threatens a horrible death for all those with Sybok, who now acknowledges that this is his own doing, the result of his own arrogance. To spare the others, Sybok, who has previously demonstrated great empathic powers, offers to take the pain of the being, who bonds with Sybok and destroys him in the process. This gives the *Enterprise* just enough time to fire a photon torpedo, damaging the stone "temple" and having at least some deleterious effect on the being. Now, however, the being, who initially wanted to merge with the *Enterprise*, manages to merge with the shuttle, preventing the return of the away team. Scotty is able to beam up Spock and McCoy, but Kirk remains stranded on the planet's surface. In a clever (if predictable) subplot twist, Klingons in pursuit of Kirk are compelled to facilitate his rescue.

In a final scene during a celebratory reception, Kirk, Spock, and Bones reflect on the events of the film, thereby offering an interpretation of the entire quest for God.

> Kirk: Cosmic thoughts, gentlemen?
> Bones: We were just speculating. . . . Is God really out there?
> Kirk: Maybe he's not out there, Bones. Maybe he's right here in the human heart.

In the remaining scenes, theological and cosmological questions receive no further consideration.

The Final Frontier suggests important stances about not only the existence of God but also the very search for God, the human condition, authentic human existence, and perhaps religion itself. The film's stance on God and traditional Terran cosmologies and theology is also quite obvious. Several centuries into the future, human myths of a primal place from which life first sprang as the result of the creative activity of an omniscient, omnipotent being persist, although such myths have fallen into general disrepute if, that is, the crew of the *Enterprise* is representative. The crew accepts Sybok's claims that such a place exists only after they have experienced his strange healing powers (powers that he claims come not from himself but from within the individual healed). These beliefs, we learn, are by no means unique to Terran culture, but they turn out to be shared by all the cultures featured in this film—Terran, Romulan, and Klingon. Each culture posits such a primal place, with its own specific name, and the existence of a supreme deity, although some of the details may vary.

The film gives no indication that the image of shared fundamental cosmology might be problematic or culture-bound by definition; neither does it seem to recognize that such a cosmology constructs Western religious beliefs as representative of all Terran culture, itself homogenized. (The Terran name for the paradisial place, after all, is given as Eden.) Underneath this image, then, is the claim that all religion is fundamentally similar, reflecting a basic reality that intelligent beings might perceive somewhat differently. This claim is projected for not only all humans but also all intelligent beings in the universe.

The Final Frontier appears equally unselfconscious about its presentation of God, at least for a film produced and released in the late 1980s. It is fascinating that when Sybok finally acknowledges that the object of his quest is "God," no one in the twenty-third century questions the terminology or its referent. When Sybok's very next words presume the masculinity of God, no one blinks, and no one articulates any discomfort when Sybok not only asserts that "my vision is from God" but also that "*he* waits for me there" (emphasis added).

The initial appearance of God draws heavily on Western scriptural imagery—the initial cataclysmic events, the fire, the wind, the voice itself. This was intentional; Shatner initially envisioned an explicitly biblical scene, with God surrounded by beings he describes as angels and cherubim that morph into monstrous gargoyles, but it apparently proved too costly. The fact that the voice is male also comes as no surprise. After the voice welcomes the travelers and McCoy asks whether it is the voice of God, the response corresponds to the implicit theology manifest earlier: Multiple religious beliefs reflect an underlying singular reality—one voice with many faces. We then see a multiplicity of those faces, apparently corresponding to the images of various interstellar cultures. But unremarkably, all those faces are recognizably humanoid and male, at least by Terran cues of gender difference. The final face we see is one remarkably familiar from Western Christian art—an old male with white hair and beard and features reflecting a distinct Semitic stereotype—the sort of picture found on many religious books for children. The fact that no one present—from the crew of the *Enterprise* to the ragtag followers of Sybok—registers any surprise at this image, or any suspicion that the image itself is troubling, is again noteworthy.

Although we can criticize the film's failure to recognize its own projection of cultural specificity, part of its failure stems from the fact that the filmmakers' concerns lie elsewhere, namely, in the falsification of all these religious claims. In the end, of course, the being is hardly God but simply another powerful, arrogant, and malevolent being who lies in wait for perhaps equally arrogant, but certainly less powerful and definitely foolish, beings through whom to wreak havoc on the rest of the universe. In Shatner's original conception the being *was* the devil rather than God, but Roddenberry objected to such explicit identifications, resulting in the generically malicious being we now see. And, of course, the film is more interested in asserting the stance articulated by Kirk—and, ironically, by the being itself—than in critiquing its own assumptions that specific human religious traditions and images may easily be projected onto the rest of intelligent life in the universe.

Gods Who Might Be

If Vaal was just a machine, the Greek gods interstellar travelers in need of a little love and groveling, Ardra a clever pretender, and the Voice of Sha Ka Ree a malicious galactic bully, not all candidates for divinity can be so quickly dismissed. *Star Trek: Deep Space Nine* offers two tantalizing possibilities: the Prophets revered by the scientifically and technologically sophisticated inhabitants of Bajor (around which the space station orbits); and the shape-shifting Founders worshiped by the Vorta and the Jem'Hadar of the imperialistic Dominion. Station security chief Odo is the Founder known most to viewers, and Odo himself is explicitly skeptical of the divine nature of his people.

The Prophets of Bajor are said to inhabit a celestial temple and to have sent the Bajoran people ten celestial orbs, which when opened afford the devotee a so-called orb experience— one's past, present, and future in some significant but obscured mystical encounter. The Prophets are believed to communicate occasionally with individual Bajorans and to reveal to select persons cryptic and ambiguous prophecies that require considerable skill to decode.

The inaugural two-part episode, "Emissary," made clear that the Prophets exist outside of linear time and are able to exist simultaneously in the past, present, and future. When Commander Benjamin Sisko first encounters these beings and gains some sense of their extraordinary abilities to negotiate time, he is initially skeptical of their identity and resistant to the suggestion of the Bajoran supreme religious leader, Kai Opaka, that Sisko might be their long-awaited emissary.

Of all the candidates for gods encountered so far, the Prophets are perhaps the most ambiguously perceptible. The audience knows they're real—but not even their emissary, Sisko, can compel them to manifest themselves. They do so only on their own terms, appearing to Sisko and eventually to others in the guise of familiar persons.

The Founders are worshiped as gods by the Vorta, beings they have created or at least modified precisely for such purposes. One episode of *Deep Space Nine* narrated a creation myth of the Vorta explaining why the Founders elevated the Vorta from their ancient primitive state to their current elevated status in the Dominion, a powerful empire in the Gamma Quadrant now threatening the Federation. Several other episodes highlight the tensions inherent in claims of these two religious systems. Consider this exchange between the Founders' majordomo, Weyoun, and a Cardassian leader, Damar, in "Tears of the Prophets":

> Weyoun: Pah-wraiths and Prophets. All this talk of gods strikes
>   me as nothing more than superstitious nonsense.
> Damar: You believe that the Founders are gods, don't you?
> Weyoun: That's different.
> Damar: In what way?
> Weyoun: The Founders *are* gods.

Although many episodes are standard Star Trek fare devoid of religious implication, the overarching plot of *Deep Space Nine* transformed into a religious drama. The concluding episodes of the show ("What You Leave Behind, Parts I and II," aired June 1999) centered on a battle of good and evil between the Bajoran Prophets and the fallen Pah-wraiths enacted as a cosmic combat between the wraith-possessed former Cardassian leader Gul Dukat and the predestined emissary of the Prophets, Benjamin Sisko (we'll return to this scenario at greater length in Chapter 2). In episodes where dependence on Terran religious tradition became obvious, we learned that Sisko's birth was arranged by the Prophets. His human mother, Sarah Sisko, was temporarily inhabited by a Prophet, who caused her to marry Sisko's father for the purpose of conceiving the Emissary. (When the Prophet departed from Sarah Sisko after Benjamin's birth, Sarah left her husband, having lost her attraction to him or, perhaps, having wondered why she had married him in the first place.) In an elegant twist on the incarnation of Jesus, Sisko is thus the son of a human father and a divine mother and a redeemer whose descent into Hell saves humanity (see also the discussion of this theme in Chapter 6).

While disqualifying the Founders offered no final resolution of the possibility that the Prophets *are* gods, if not God, "Favor the Bold" strongly suggests that Weyoun's retort to Damar ("The Founders *are* gods") was seriously mistaken on both counts. If it did not completely resolve the question of the divinity of the Prophets, it certainly demonstrated their extraordinary power and ability to intervene in the conflict between the Federation and the Dominion in a way that seems miraculous by Terran standards. Having failed to staunch the Dominion advance, a desperate Sisko implores the Prophets: "You want to be gods—then *be* gods. I need a miracle. Bajor needs a miracle. Stop those ships [from coming through the Wormhole]." And they do. Moreover, the actions of the Founders, including their relationship with the destructive, if not demonic, Dominion, coupled with their illness and imminent death from a lethal virus planted by Federation covert operatives, would seem to undermine Weyoun's claim.

In the Star Trek universe, then, divinity and mortality are not mutually exclusive (in fact, the Klingon gods died eons ago at the hands of ancient Klingon warriors: "They were more trouble than they were worth," according to Worf in *Deep Space Nine's* "Homefront," aired January 1996). Potential deities are also disproportionately male. This is certainly true for self-cast characters like Apollo, the god of the Edo (*Next Generation*'s "Justice," aired November 1987), the Caretaker, as well as the omnipotent Q (a character we consider below who never shows up in drag despite his fondness for disguises). But it's also true for humans mistakenly taken for gods, like Picard and the comical Ferengi, who briefly pass themselves off as divine in *Deep Space Nine*'s "Body Parts" (aired June 1996). Still, the Star Trek writers explore the traditions surrounding female deities: The powerful mythic *Next Generation* episode "Masks" (aired February 1994) features two balancing powers, the solar female Masaka and the lunar male Korgano, in perpetual chase of one another. But it is one thing to acknowledge that other cultures envision the divine as male and female, another to consider the possibility that God might indeed be female. The obvious fraud is one thing: Imaging Ardra as female fits well with numerous Terran traditions of the alluring but dangerous woman. (Even the amorphous, unattractive female Founder who commands the Dominion forces in later *Deep Space Nine* episodes may also conform to this paradigm.)

The point is that the characters whose claim to divinity cannot be dismissed out of hand are likely to be male, with a few exceptions. The Bajoran Prophets, for instance, seem willing to animate the images of women and men when they manifest as corporeal beings. The Prophets, in fact, pose an interesting dilemma: If gender is somehow related to having a body, it seems difficult to understand how the Prophets could be gendered. If, however, gender is not inherent in the body but rather in culturally constructed roles, then perhaps the Prophets could be gendered after all (although not in a biological, sexual way).

And then there is the Borg Queen. She exhibits characteristics of the divine, more so than we might understand at first glance. Our first encounter with the Borg Queen is in the film *Star Trek: First Contact*:

> I am the beginning, the end, the one who is many.
> I am the Borg.
> I am the collective.
> I bring order to Chaos.

Contrast this pronouncement to the following lines from a hymn to the Egyptian goddess Isis, worshiped throughout the Mediterranean world during the Roman period:

> I am Isis, the mistress of every land. . . .
> I gave and ordained laws for men, which no one is able to change
> I divided the earth from the heaven
> I showed the path of the stars
> I ordered the course of the sun and the moon. . . .
> I ordained that the true should be thought good. . . .
> I am the Queen of rivers and wind and sea. . . .
> I am the Queen of war. . . .
> I overcome Fate.

And then consider these lines, uttered by a female speaker from a work sometimes called *Thunder: Perfect Mind*, found among the so-called Nag Hammadi library in Egypt:

> I am the first and the last
> I am the honored one and the scored one
> I am the whore and the holy one. . . .

I am lust in (outward) appearance,
and interior self-control exists within me.

Such language is not unique to female deities: It is found in
the speech of the male god Krishna in the *Bhagavad Gita*, in
the language of the Apocalypse of John (the book of Revelation), and the words of Jesus in the canonical New Testament
Gospel of John.

In ancient Mediterranean sources, such formal pronouncement language—phrases typically beginning with the words "I
am"—signaled the divinity of the speaker and a recital of divine attributes. The structure and content of the Borg Queen's
pronouncement suggest she is to be taken as a divine figure.
Yet viewers recoil at her ghastly appearance, which conjures
images from the darkest recesses of the human unconscious.
The Borg themselves may be understood to symbolize our fear
of artificial beings—part machine, part biological life-form—
whose purpose is to annihilate all that is human. At least in
Western thought, individuality is crucial to our self-understanding, and the Borg represent the antithesis—a collective
with no individual will. Surely, the Borg Queen, like the Borg
collective, is more an exemplar of perfect evil than of God. At
best, does she not represent the devil?

Our resistance to viewing the Borg Queen as divine may lie
in the confluence of her gender, sexuality, power, and compelling appearance. Played by Alice Krige, the Borg Queen
possesses arrogance and confidence and, like the simultaneously mothering and destroying goddesses of Hinduism and
other traditions, manages to be sexually arousing and visually
repulsive. She manifests other characteristics of Terran deities:
She is extraordinarily powerful, prescient if not omniscient,
knowing of the minds of others. She may be immortal, for she

apparently survived the destruction of the Borg vessel in *Next Generation's* "The Best of Both Worlds" (in which she does not actually appear as a character; her presence is assumed in the plot of *First Contact*). She displays tantalizing affinities with goddesses of life, death, sexuality, and destruction from Terran traditions (goddesses whom some contemporary interpreters have seen as cultural expressions of male fears about women who pretend to nurture but secretly aspire to destroy).

In the end, however, she is merely a flawed representation of false gods, although on a different order than, say, Ardra, whose claims to divinity are deluded and expedient. She even stands head and shoulders above the demonic being in *Star Trek V: The Final Frontier*, whose extraordinary powers are insufficient to qualify as divine. Still, like virtually every divine pretender with the possible exception of Q, she constitutes another threat to human existence that must ultimately be overcome. It may not be accidental that her confident pronouncement not only echoes the language of Jesus in the Gospel of John but also evokes the feminine divine in "marginalized" polytheist and gnostic traditions.

Star Trek's most intriguing candidate for divinity remains Q, played by actor John de Lancie. Q assumed central roles in the inaugural and concluding episodes of *Next Generation* ("Encounter at Farpoint" and "All Good Things . . . ") and throughout the series. Despite the crew's irritation at the appearance of Q and its consistent refusal to treat him (and the Q Continuum) as anything but an annoying, perplexing life-form, Q displays the core attributes of God in Western monotheist traditions: omniscience, omnipotence, and immortality. Despite these attributes, *Next Generation* never explicitly affirms Q's divinity. Instead, numerous episodes including Q draw upon narratives of encounters between humans and the divine, particularly those found in Jewish and Christian Scriptures.

In "Hide and Q," for instance, Q gives First Officer William Riker his own extraordinary powers and tells him to use them. The encounter between Q and Riker plays on Christian themes of temptation and incarnation—beginning with the serpent's temptation of the primordial humans in Genesis. What Q offers Riker is essentially what the serpent offers Eve and Adam—knowledge and, by extension, immortality. In Genesis 3:4, the serpent says to Eve: "You will not die [when you eat the fruit of the tree of knowledge of good and evil]; for God knows that when you eat of it your eyes will be opened, and you will be like God, knowing good and evil." In Genesis 3:22, the real assault on the divine is more obvious: "Then the LORD God said, 'See, the [human] has become like one of us, knowing good and evil; and now, he might reach out his hand and take also from the tree of life, and eat, and live forever." For fear of this, God expels Adam and Eve from the Garden.

By offering Riker knowledge and immortality, Q does what the serpent does; indeed he goes farther, conferring powers upon Riker without his acquiescence. In this sense, Riker is hardly Adam, as he does not choose to reach beyond what he has been given. Instead, he has "greatness thrust upon" him, and what Riker does next bears a striking resemblance to narratives of Jesus in the canonical gospels (see, e.g., Matt 11:4–6, paralleled in Luke 7:22–23): He gives sight to the blind (Geordi La Forge), gives humanity to Data, and resurrects members of the crew who have died in a battle staged by Q. He discerns the true state of human and Klingon souls, perceiving and granting Worf's desires for a mate. Such deeds do not point unambiguously to Jesus (some might think instead of the Wizard of Oz, who gave a brain to the Scarecrow, a heart to the Tin Man, and courage to the Cowardly Lion), but many viewers are likely to make this connection.

The representation of Riker as Jesus continues in a series of scenes in which Riker struggles with the temptation to assume his newfound powers permanently and use them in a godlike manner. He actually says to Picard, "No one has offered to turn me into a god before." At least from Riker's point of view, Q is offering him divinity, and since these powers are those of the Q Continuum itself, one easily drawn conclusion is that the Q are themselves divine.

In a continuing play on Christian referents, Q appears suddenly on the bridge, "draped in what is recognizable, even in this century, as the somber robes of something like the Franciscan holy order . . . playing it to the hilt with gentle voice, kindliness shining from his face, fingers pointed together as in prayer" (from the *Star Trek Script* series, *Book One: The Q Chronicles* [New York: Simon and Schuster, 1998], p. 167). Facing the bridge crew, he inaugurates the following exchange:

> Q: Let us pray for understanding, let us pray for compassion, and for—
> Picard [interrupting]: Let us do no such damn thing.
> Q [holding up a cross]: I forgive you your blasphemy.

"Hide and Q" plays on conflicts between humans and divine beings narrated in many religious traditions—with some twists. In many myths, it is humans who seek the powers of the divine, the gods who seek to repel and rebuff them. In "Hide and Q," ironically, an arguably divine being seeks to give humans divine powers, and the humans in the end make the wise decision to decline the corruption that such powers constitute. Many interpreters of religion see mythological conflicts between humans and gods as analogies for conflicts between adolescents and adults—the son dethroning the father; the next generation deposing the authority of the present generation. Although the writers of Star Trek may not have given this question much thought, it is appropriate that the male Q plays the role of God and the macho first officer contemplates becoming divine. Accordingly, we might question whether such stories adequately reflect the transitions to adulthood that girls experience or whether they adequately reflect daughter-mother conflicts. How "universal" is this depiction?

It's worth pointing out that psychologists of religion have illuminated the degree to which universal (or at least presumably universal) human experiences, particularly childhood and maturation, play a role in the formation of human religious imagery for the divine. They suggest that humans often project the infant-parent relationship onto the divine realm and onto the divine/human relationship. Some of this, of course, may be transparently obvious in the prevalence of parental imagery for God, imagery that in Western monotheistic traditions becomes almost exclusively paternal. Numerous studies have considered the degree to which the powers ascribed to the divine, and the feelings of the worshipper in relation to the divine, are related or analogous to the powers of the parent (or authority figure) and the feelings of the infant toward the parent.

Despite numerous allusions to Q's divinity, objections can be raised to the suggestion. Q's behavior in "Hide and Q" and other episodes might appear inconsistent with the Western concept of God as wholly good. In many appearances Q is comic, provoking Picard, Riker, Worf, and even Janeway (in *Voyager*) to exasperation. He appears playful ("Like a master and a beloved pet," as Data observes in "All Good Things . . . "), but there is an agenda after all. Whatever the *Enterprise* characters seek— power, love, freedom, the ability to change the past—Q demonstrates that their understanding is limited (although, as he says to Riker in "Hide and Q," human potential may not be). This is precisely the function of the Trickster, the figure we know from Native American tradition and other cultures. And at least one Star Trek writer conceptualized Q as the Norse mythic figure Loki (a mischief-maker; among other things, he intentionally brings about the death of the beautiful and beloved god Balder).

The Trickster often appears in serious religious contexts, such as ritual, to reverse expectations, inject humor as a foil for realization, or tease the faithful to exasperation in order to achieve a higher level of understanding. The Trickster will often use an androgynous persona, cross-dressing or affecting mannerisms appropriate to the opposite gender in that particular culture. In the many episodes when Q seems bent on achieving the ridiculous, what he finally achieves is a shift in perspective. Although the use of humor in religious contexts is largely alien to mainstream American religious traditions, it is acceptable practice in many Terran religions. When he himself is banished from the Q Continuum for his tricks in *Next Generation's* "Deja Q," Q is in fact enacting a timeless formula, for the Trickster is, by definition, over the edge: He walks the line between the acceptable and unacceptable and oversteps the boundary, in the process calling into question the rightness of such boundaries.

Although the representation of Q as a Trickster may not accord well with Western views of the divine, in many traditions tricksters are part of the divine pantheon. Thus, Q's penchant for trickery does not derail his candidacy for divinity.

Alternatively, we might see Q as a kind of spiritual enabler. From his initial goading appearance in "Encounter at Farpoint" to the ultimate test he foists upon Picard in "All Good Things . . ." Q ultimately serves to guide humanity on its evolutionary journey to higher forms of self-understanding and actualization. In this capacity, Q is not far from the Jewish and Christian tradition of the divinely approved satanic tempter. There is another possibility. If Q is not God, then his character represents Western notions of God, functioning as a device through which the Star Trek writers can explore and critique those same notions. Regardless of whether Q is God or the divine adversary or something else, we need not be cowed by him or his formidable powers.

Q's relationship with Picard, and with the *Enterprise* crew, bookends *Next Generation*. "Encounter at Farpoint" inaugurates a trial of humanity on charges of violence and hubris that is only temporarily suspended. The reconvened trial in "All Good Things . . ." implies that the seven-year journey of the next generation had been about humanity's encounter with Q, a test of cosmic and mythic proportions. Q's announcement to an aggravated Picard that the "trial never ends" suggests that humanity is to be continually judged. When Picard reacts by insisting that it is not for Q "to set the standard by which we shall be judged," Q responds, "Ah, but it is . . . and we have. You are guilty. Humanity will be destroyed." "All Good Things . . ." thus presents Picard with a final test, one that will determine human existence.

In the end, Q suggests to Picard that human capabilities are beyond our present imaginings and that we squander that potential far too easily, just as the *Enterprise* has failed in the seven years since the journey to Farpoint to change and grow. He tells Picard that change and growth are "the exploration that awaits you: not mapping stars and studying nebula, but charting the unknowable possibilities of existence."

Q's suggestion—that the secret and the mystery of human existence lie within ourselves, rather than "out there"—is a familiar mystic insight in Terran traditions. Our proclivity to project onto others (and into space) that which resides within ourselves, and thus miss true understanding, has been explored especially in the meditative traditions of Asia.

The closing image of "All Good Things . . ." is that of circles, repeatedly displayed: the circle of playing cards on the circular table in the circular saucer of the ship in the vastness of space, which might itself be circular, or spiraled, like the galaxy. Circles are not the image of choice in mainstream Western cultural and religious tradition, which prefers linear portrayals of time (a single creation and a single destruction); linear and text-oriented progressions from the primitive to the sublime; the "straight and narrow" path to perfection or salvation or even oblivion. But from India to China to Japan, the circle is the predominant image of choice. Traditional as well as contemporary teachings in Sanatana Dharma (Hindu) traditions view creation and destruction as infinitely cyclical. From the Hindu and Buddhist mandalas beyond number, to the yin-yang symbol of the Tao, to the Shinto image of the rising sun, the circle is historically the dominant manifestation of ultimate reality.

Q's role in "All Good Things . . ." ultimately forces us to preface any conclusions we might draw about a human-divine relationship. Q, after all, gives Picard the helping hand to counter the directive given by the Q Continuum, provided Picard can grasp the fundamental paradox that lies at the center of the double episode. The ability to deal with such a paradox, it is suggested, might cause us to grow and reverse the judgment of a higher authority. Whether Q's assistance should be read as evidence of his true role as *psychopomp* (see Chapter 3), or as a clue to his divine care for humans, or perhaps even something else, is never clear. What is clear, however, is that Q has great concern for the survival of humanity, risking the wrath of the Continuum to shepherd Picard through a maze of apparent contradictions in order to save humanity.

So *Is* There God in the Universe?

There are many powerful beings in the Star Trek universe, including some, like Q, whose abilities and characteristics closely approximate Terran conceptions of divinity. Such beings are sometimes taken for gods by less powerful and knowledgeable species. But if "God" means some kind of Western monotheist notion, then there is no ultimate God in the Star Trek universe. The difference between humans and divine beings may be one of degree, not of kind, and the closest candidate for divinity, Q, recognizes and perhaps fears precisely that. The words of God to the divine court in Genesis 3:22 (concerning the human being) could, with little alteration, have been spoken by Q and the Continuum at the close of "All Good Things . . . ": "See, the man has become like one of us, knowing good and evil; and now, he might reach out his hand and take also from the tree of life, and eat, and live forever." Whereas in Genesis and in "Encounter at Farpoint" such a prospect evokes concern, if not anxiety, on the part of the speaker, in "All Good Things . . ." Q is relieved, even optimistic about the ability of humanity to transcend its flaws and limitations and achieve its full potential.

What Evil Lurks
Beyond the Stars?

WILLIAM CASSIDY

This chapter looks at the forces of evil in the Star Trek universe. Accordingly, we start with the simple question "What is evil?" Given the necessity of conflict as a central element in heroic tales in general, and TV-episode plots in particular, there are plenty of bad guys in Star Trek. But there's not a lot of evil. Western scholars use several meanings for the term. There is *natural* evil: disastrous events like floods, earthquakes, and stellar novas that harm people but are understood as results of physical processes rather than of conscious intentionality. There is *moral* evil, understood as intentional acts done by sentient beings, acts that contravene established standards.

When moral evil is linked to the notion that the universe is divided into two opposed principles, one of which is good, the other evil, then we have *cosmic* evil. Cosmic evil is associated with the infernal powers, such as Satan in Christian mythology or the Zoroastrian being Ahriman, who are at war with the powers of good. Then there is *metaphysical* evil, caused not by agents existing in the universe but by the lack of perfection of the universe itself. The distinction between cosmic and metaphysical evil depends on whether evil is associated with active supernatural personalities or due to imperfections in the blueprint of the universe.

Because concepts of evil were developed primarily by philosophers and theologians in Western civilization, they should have some bearing on the universe of Star Trek, created, as it is, by North Americans. The view that tends to dominate our culture, whether explicitly or implicitly, is that of cosmic evil. Although cosmic evil is fundamental to Christianity, even secular culture tends to embrace this dichotomizing of experience into categories of good and evil. Thus, it may come as a surprise to find that even though Star Trek is full of disasters and villains, we don't find that these situations generally correspond to the senses of evil developed in Western culture, particularly cosmic evil.

The treatment of the Klingons in the Original Series and *Next Generation* provides a good example of the Star Trek approach. In the Original Series, Klingons were the quintessential bad guys: violent, aggressive, a truly evil empire—the model of cosmic evil—a fundamental opposition to the Federation, its aims, and its philosophy. This enemy alien species comes to a rapprochement with the Federation only in *Star Trek VI: The Undiscovered Country*. In a *Next Generation* episode from the first season, "Heart of Glory," which takes place after

Undiscovered Country in the Star Trek chronology, some renegade Klingons are rescued by the *Enterprise* crew and meet the Starfleet officer Worf, who is eager to get to know them. There is an existing treaty between the Klingon Empire and the Federation, but they are not trusting friends. Two Klingons (a third dies on the *Enterprise* of battle wounds) see a kindred spirit in Worf (a Klingon raised by Terrans). The Klingons embrace Worf as a brother whose heart is that of a hunter and a warrior even though he has been raised by a race of weaklings. Worf is intrigued, almost enchanted by the encounter. He, too, feels a strong kinship, and this leads to a conflict as the plot develops: Will he betray Starfleet to save his new comrades?

Of course he doesn't (honor is paramount to Worf), but he does solve a dilemma by arranging for the last Klingon to die in battle, in a manner consonant with Klingon values. Actually it is Worf who kills him and then performs the Klingon death ritual, ensuring an honorable end for this all-too-brief acquaintance. Worf meets his Klingon roots and successfully grafts onto them. His embrace of these roots is so thorough that he is told by the commander of the Klingon warbird looking for the renegades that he should join up with the Empire when his tour with the *Enterprise* is completed.

Worf, of course, remains to serve on the *Enterprise*. So what does this story have to do with evil? In the Original Series the Klingons were evil, alien enemies—the aggressively destructive antithesis of all that the Federation represented. By *Next Generation* they're no longer enemies, and they're not evil. Even the appearance of the Klingons is modified in *Next Generation*. The valuation of the empire is changed, just like the makeup for the actors. So is the way the writers treat them, a shift well in line with the general Star Trek mode of dealing with aliens. In *Next Generation* we come to know the Klingons and gain a deeper appreciation of their culture. Although they're still violent and aggressive, we now understand it is in their nature. Our consciousness has been raised; we now have a clearer view. It's not that they're evil, they're just different. Their values may not track the Federation's, but they are valid and coherent. Klingons revere warrior values, and while Federation folks may consider these customs rather quaint or even primitive, that doesn't make them evil.

Terran religions (to move from imaginative Star Trek reality back to our own earthbound time and place) hardly agree as to the existence of evil as an inherent principle in the universe. The dominant view of Western culture is Christian—*cosmic evil*: The world is divided up into two camps, the good and the bad. The forces of the good follow God and seek righteousness but are opposed in this world by the minions of Satan who would thwart God's plan for goodness. This world, then, is the place of battle between absolute good and absolute evil, a battle in which there can be no neutrality. You're either part of the problem or part of the solution.

Most of us in the Western world are influenced by this myth, even if we don't believe it. Religious myths (many scholars claim that there are secular myths as well) usually tell stories about the deeds of powerful supernatural beings that determine the ways both the natural world and human society function. Scholars often extend the term "myth" to include the more abstract ideas and points of view that are embedded in the cultural fabric. Obviously the myths of one culture will differ from the myths of another, although we find many thematic parallels.

In history, we first identify this mythology of a cosmic division of reality into good and evil, which religionists also call "ethical dualism," in the Persian religion of Zoroastrianism, which was well-established in the Persian empire half a millennium before the time of Jesus. The founder of this faith was the Prophet Zarathustra (Zoroaster is the Greek form of his name), who, according to the revelations he received from Ahura Mazda, the Wise Lord and One True God, saw the world as divided into the Followers of the Truth and the Followers of the Lie, who are inspired by Ahriman the Evil One. We are free to choose between these two camps, but choose we must, and the stakes are enormous. The righteous will find a heavenly reward while the wicked will be afflicted with everlasting torment in the House of the Lie.

This powerful way of thinking about good and evil may have been something new in the world at that moment and had profound influence on views found in Judaism, Christianity, and Islam. This myth is one of the root metaphors in Western thought for considering the relationship of good and evil in the world. It's like a default mode for us—but it's not the only way to think about good and evil. In fact, it does not appear to be the primary way in which Star Trek approaches the issue.

Top Guns for the Evil One

Anyone who has spent much time in front of the tube watching Star Trek knows that the episodes are full of villains. Conflict is necessary to plot development, and the shows are in the adventure genre, Gene Roddenberry's *Wagon Train* to the stars. But where is theological evil? Absolute evil? Cosmic evil? Below we consider some candidates for possible nomination to the Intergalactic League of Satan.

Everybody who liked the *Enterprise* chief of security in *Next Generation*, Tasha Yar, was shocked when she was suddenly killed (and not resurrected) in the first-season episode "Skin of Evil." None of the central crew was killed in the Original Series. Even Spock, who died in *Star Trek II: The Wrath of Khan*, was regenerated in *Star Trek III: The Search for Spock* and is still going (underground on Romulus) at last report. Tasha was a great character, cast across stereotypical gender expectations as a female chief of security, played by Denise Crosby as very tough and serious, but nevertheless quite appealing. She even had a fling with Data, but then she's killed during an away mission. This was not an expendable ensign, for Tasha Yar was part of the ensemble, a known quantity. And her death is not depicted as particularly heroic: It seems rather accidental and meaningless (later confirmed in "Yesterday's Enterprise").

The monster who kills Tasha might seem a good nominee for Evil One in the Star Trek universe. Its name is Armus, and it looks like an animated tarpit, an alien so nasty that his fellow aliens imprisoned him on an isolated planet. Had ship's counselor Deanna Troi not crash-landed a shuttle near his tarpit, thereby providing a hostage, Tasha might have blocked any chances for her subordinate Worf's promotion for years to come. The *Enterprise* happens upon the planet; odious monster that he is, Armus kills Yar.

Armus is promiscuously malignant, and he takes on the role of a hated enemy to our heroes, but his power is much too limited for him to be taken seriously. He is stuck on the planet, which can be quarantined. He doesn't have the magnitude to be evil (he's only mean). Then, too, he seems to have had a deprived childhood; there are reasons why he is so antisocial. In Star Trek, we can usually find a psychological or social reason—sometimes a biological one—to explain sociopathic behavior.

Another candidate appears in the Original Series' second-season episode "Wolf in the Fold," but this one is far more mobile, having moved through time and space for centuries from Earth to other planets, always killing innocent women. The earliest recorded incarnation seems to have been Jack the Ripper, but the crew discovers a trail of bloody murders throughout subsequent history. This nasty creature is now possessing chief engineer Scotty, and it takes a seance (no less) to sort things out. Spock suggests that the culprit is a bodiless entity that derives nourishment from the fear of its victims, whom it attacks and kills while possessing their bodies. Captain Kirk and company get rid of the alien by forcing it into the dead body of its former host and transporting it into space. This entity is certainly horrible from the human perspective, feeding, as it were, on human terror, but we can hardly link it to cosmic evil. It is not part of any cosmic opposition, and in a sense its only problem is that it has rather nasty table habits. It must be sent out of the dining room and up to its own room as a punishment. Permanently.

Two members of the race of aliens from Devidia II provide candidates when they take human form and disguise themselves as characters known as Doctor Apollinaire and the Nurse. These mysterious, rather demonic figures make their appearance in Next Generation's two-part, season-spanning episode, "Time's Arrow," which takes us to San Francisco in the time of Mark Twain. The plot is complicated and doesn't really concern us here; it suffices to explain that the aliens are from the twenty-fourth century and have traveled to nineteenth-century San Francisco to steal neural energy from humans in order to ship it back to Devidia II, where the energy is apparently an important source of nourishment. But these vampirish creatures are sucking up our life's source, and Picard and crew have to do something. Set as it is on nineteenth-century Earth, the episode evokes associations with Bram Stoker's novel *Dracula*, and the Devidians' choice of nourishment parallels that of the renowned vampire.

As the plot ensues, Doctor Apollinaire and the Nurse are discovered and forced to flee. He escapes back to Devidia II through a portal, but the Nurse is killed. Of course, after many twists the Federation once again is able to make the universe safe for human neural energy sources. Once the crew returns safely to the twenty-fourth century, the *Enterprise* blows Devidia II to smithereens with photon torpedoes. So much for the Prime Directive, but we may be sure they would have done the same to Armus if he had presented a similar threat.

Again, we could ask just where good and evil lie in this scenario. Clearly, the Devidians, like the formless alien in "Wolf in the Fold," might have a different answer from that of the Federation team. One man's meat is another man's neural energy (or fear), it seems. But in contrast to the case of the Klingons, in these episodes there is no talk of treaties. Here the enemies are simply eliminated. Again, as with Armus, the Devidian II aliens seem rather more mundane; they lack magnitude. Dracula, in contrast, was a villain that, as conceived by Bram Stoker and countless others, was satanic, in league with the cosmic opposition, Evil's agent in Victorian London. Although garlic would do in a pinch, the best vampire repellent was a cross, which expresses the cosmic nature of this evil in Christian terms. The Devidian aliens are simply another race going about its economic business, ruthlessly exploiting the resources of an alien (Third World?) planet—nineteenth-century Earth. The model here seems to be more one of technologically superior *free enterprise* than of cosmic evil. The terror-eating alien also has his own food habits, to which we object. But this, too, is hardly a case of Cosmic Evil.

"Devil's Due," a *Next Generation* episode from the fourth season, provides an interesting character. Ardra is apparently the devil to the people of planet Ventax II. She struck a Mephistophelian bargain to provide a thousand years of peace; at the end of the millennium the descendants would all become her slaves—and time's up! Ardra is a beautiful young woman attracted to Picard, spicing up the episode, and her superpowers of transformation and translocation lend credence to her claim to be the Princess of Darkness. Her claim is substantiated by the actual contract, which is retrieved from the Ventaxian archives. As eligible as the female Satan would be for our purposes, she, too, must be rejected. It's all a con.

A more intriguing scenario arises when the *Next Generation* crew becomes the subject of a scientific experiment in the episode "Where Silence Has Lease." The starship becomes caught in a spatial trap of neither energy nor matter—in fact, the trap doesn't exist in any normal physical sense. Nevertheless, they are stuck. There is an abandoned starship nearby, which they investigate, only to be faced with a series of strange incidents, rather like a test-rat in a maze. Eventually they are confronted by an alien being, Nagilum, which seems to have the form of a huge human eye. It is interested in studying the way humans die and proposes to use part of the crew for experimental purposes. This may remind the viewer of mad-scientist matinees, but Nagilum is hardly insane, merely interested in an abstract, unemotional way. Although he is not in the least concerned by the pathos of individual human suffering, he does have a scientific interest in the phenomena that surround human death. Picard decides that he has but one countermove in his power, and a difficult choice it is: He begins the ship's autodestruct sequence, preferring to destroy the ship and crew than to sit by while his people are killed one by one.

With only a few seconds before self-oblivion, the *Enterprise* returns to normal space. Picard terminates the autodestruct sequence. Nagilum reports that he has learned much about human nature. What began as a dreadful, nightmarish experiment and continues as a chess match with catastrophe ends calmly, with Picard's characteristically sang-froid remark that human beings and Nagilum share a common characteristic: curiosity.

The final candidate for our list is the archvillain of the Sherlock Holmes stories, the evil Professor Moriarty, as author Arthur Conan Doyle often called him. Commander Data is an avid reader of Conan Doyle's nineteenth-century tales of the logical Holmes, and so he creates a holodeck program based on the stories. But Data's buddy Geordi La Forge complains that Data already knows all the stories, so there isn't any problem-solving challenge, any mystery, in the program. So Geordi asks the computer to make it harder by creating an adversary in the Sherlock Holmes program who would be an equal to the cyborg Data. That adversary is Professor Moriarty, but this computer-generated Moriarty is more than a match for Data's Sherlock Holmes—and nearly a match for all the resources that the *Enterprise* crew can muster.

Moriarty becomes conscious (as will other programs, e.g., the Sinatra-like crooner Vic Fontaine in *Deep Space Nine* and the holographic Doctor in *Voyager*) and thus becomes a life-form, although one limited to a cyber existence. And, of course, he has the character of the brilliant villain immortalized by Conan Doyle; the archenemy of Holmes, Moriarty is the evil spider at the center of nineteenth-century London's crime web. As played by Daniel Davis in two episodes of *Next Generation*, Doctor Moriarty is one of the most memorable minor characters in the entire series. Sardonic and gallant in the episode "Elementary, Dear Data," he charms Doctor Katherine Pulaski while threatening the existence of the entire ship. That's easy for him, since he is a computer program and, once conscious, is able to manipulate the system in a manner that would cause any modern hacker sell his soul.

Moriarty isn't interested in destroying the ship, however, as that would be suicide; what he really wants is freedom. This proves technologically impossible, but the *Enterprise* crew can certainly appreciate his desire. After all, he's really only a rogue—hardly a minion of evil. In *Next Generation* Moriarty has a noble spirit, and in his second appearance ("Ship in a Bottle") he is motivated by his love for the beautiful Countess Regina Barthalomew. So when it becomes clear that he means no threat to the *Enterprise* if his demands are granted, the officers accommodate his wishes by moving his program to an independent computer. Moriarty and Regina, dwelling in an independent cyber universe, are free to roam its galaxy, leaving the *Enterprise* free of further disturbance.

In all of these episodes, what appears to be evil in the beginning is mediated and often defused by a scientific and humanistic perspective. None of these examples sustains any cosmic situation in which evil and good oppose one another as the primary colors in the cosmic fabric. The Star Trek universe doesn't seem to be constructed that way—in Star Trek good and evil are relativized rather than being absolutely opposed. Possible exemplars of evil—Armus, Nagilum, Ardra, et al.— who initially appear demonic wind up as isolated, individualized alien jerks, interstellar cannibals, scientists, or con artists and mere criminals. As with the Klingons treaties can be made; if no peaceful approach is forthcoming, well, the *Enterprise* crew members are resourceful. Sometimes the only good bad alien is a dead bad alien. Force is an option in the Star Trek universe.

Star Trek Versus Star Wars

Essentially, Star Trek and Star Wars are parallel universes of cinematic entertainment. Although there is much in Star Wars that might be fruitfully compared with and contrasted to Star Trek, we have chosen not to do so, for that would be another project entirely. Yet the contrast in their visions of evil is so striking that we cannot ignore George Lucas's imaginary universe. What we don't find in Star Trek's universe is the dualism so celebrated in Star Wars. In Star Trek, there is no Dark Side of the Force (indeed, there is no Force). Lucas's dualism may have been modeled on Chinese yin-yang notions in some ways, but it has equal inspiration from the Zoroastrian ethical dualism of good and evil. Both the dark (yin) and the light (yang) are present in the Force (as they are in Tao), but in Star Wars the dark is associated with evil and the light with good; in Taoism no such ethical links are made. Western ethical dualism, in contrast, denies the essential connection between good and evil that Star Wars's Force assumes. Darkness and light are the two *sides* of the Force, which makes it so intriguing to audiences, for that is something new and different. The concept of the Force, then, seems to be composed of elements derived from both Chinese and Persian religions.

Thus, the evil that seems to be absent in the Star Trek universe is part of the fabric of Star Wars, but there is a parallel in that the mythological personifications of good and evil—God and the devil—seem to be absent in both. In Star Wars, good and evil are personified in mortals: extraordinary heroes like Obi Wan and hypervillains of the Dark Side like the Emperor Palpatine. This lack of *divine* exemplars seems to be a clear and emphatic difference between the Force and Zoroastrian dualism, which opposes Ahura Mazda as God to Ahriman as devil. One can certainly picture the evil emperor in Star Wars as Satan, complete with his infernal powers, leading his faceless minions of evil such as his red-robed Imperial Guards. Darth Vader then, seems like Satan's agent, the tempter Mephistopheles, who is adept at fitting the temptation to the personality of the victim ("Luke, I am your father"). Vader, wrapped in darkness, wields the forces of evil against the earthy rebels, who represent the forces of good. But this view doesn't quite follow the script. Both the emperor and Vader are quite mortal—they're no more gods than are Luke and C3PO. Evil, yes; linked to the Dark Side, yes; but mortal human beings. (Even though Vader is a cyborg, he dies a human.)

Is the Q Continuum Star Trek's answer to the Force? Not really. First, there are individuals in the Q Continuum; it is not an impersonal cosmic force-field that other species can link into. Second, although the Q Continuum has immense powers, it's dismissive of good and evil as humans, or other species, understand them. Finally, the realm of explanation in Star Trek is scientific and technological rather than spiritual and mystical. Many beings have superhuman powers in the Star Trek universe, but those powers are generally explained scientifically. Nagilum, for instance, possessing extraordinary powers over the physical world, is modeled on a scientist rather than on a divinity. The spiritualized ethical dualism of the Force is not paralleled in Star Trek.

The Taoist Model

A parallel model for the Star Trek view does exist, but it is found in religion, not cinema sci-fi. Taoism, perhaps the most ancient Chinese spiritual philosophy, follows ancient traditions in analyzing things in the world into complementary opposites: yin and yang. Yin is dark, moist, yielding, female—to name a few characteristics—whereas yang is the opposite: bright, dry, firm, male. Things in the world are composed of both elements, but, in contrast to Zoroastrian dualism, good and evil are not part of the Taoist contrasts. Yin is not evil, or yang good. One might certainly propose a preference for yin or yang (in traditional China, Confucianism tends toward yang, Taoism toward yin), but neither is associated with the ethical categories of good and evil per se.[1]

Perhaps a story will help to clarify this Chinese view:

A farmer finds a horse. "What good luck!" says his neighbor. "Who can say how things will turn out?" replies the farmer. The next day his son is thrown from the horse and breaks his leg. "Oh, what bad luck!" remarks the neighbor, who, as you can see, is something of a busybody. "Who can say how things will turn out," replies the farmer, who has known the neighbor for forty years. A few days later, the army comes through the village on a conscription campaign. They take the neighbor's son as a recruit and also confiscate the horse, but they leave the farmer's son because of the injury. The heart-broken neighbor visits the farmer to lament the fact that sons who join the army are rarely seen again. "Who can say how things will turn out?" is once more the reply.

This Chinese way of understanding events seems to illuminate the Star Trek perspective. Thus, enemies such as the Klingons may, in time, become worthy allies, as in the last episodes of *Deep Space Nine*, where Klingon and Federation forces join in battle to defeat the Dominion. Likewise Nagilum is not, as he originally seems, a demonic torturer but an unimaginably powerful scientist who shares with us the important trait of curiosity. In this case, which supports a pervasive model in Star Trek, understanding the Other brings a more positive connection to it, as well as a shift in cognitive categories: demon to scientist.

The Taoist suspension of judgment also seems to apply to the way the writers and producers portray Q, an entity who begins as an enemy of all things human in the first episode of *Next Generation*. But Q, as mercurial as he is powerful, takes on a number of roles that have religious locations and connections.

In that inaugural episode, "Encounter at Farpoint," Q serves as judge over *Enterprise* Captain Jean-Luc Picard and humankind in general. He is as stern and merciless as that God of wrath whom hellfire-and-brimstone preachers eagerly invoke. In other episodes, such as "Hide and Q," he plays a more devilish role: Mephistopheles the tempter. Q grants Riker superhuman powers—whether as an experiment or as a test of Riker's character is not entirely clear—but it's a temptation worthy of Faust, in either case. Q also fulfills a demonic role generally, at least in the opinion of the Continuum, when he is expelled and made mortal in "Deja Q." He is a fallen angel, indeed, one brought even lower than Satan—Q is made a human being! But he redeems himself (unlike Satan) by learning from human frailty. He attempts to save the *Enterprise* crew by sacrificing himself, having learned altruism through, ironically, the example of Data, who himself desires greatly to be more human.

As with Jesus Christ, Q is reduced from an omnipotent form to a limited, human one. Becoming human, he suffers and sacrifices himself for other humans. Through this sacrifice he regains omnipotence. Although the parallels are not exact, they are intriguing. Finally, Q appears a rather humane and loving father at the end of *Voyager's* "The Q and the Gray"; he even works to make peace in the Continuum. Few characters in the Star Trek universe are more entertaining than Q, played by John de Lancie with humor and dash. Although Q often takes a villain's role as antagonist to Picard and Starfleet, he's not Satan. As "Deja Q" seems to insist, this fallen angel—by any definition a protean character who defies any simple analysis—is saved.

This point of view also explains the way that technology is presented in Star Trek. Obviously, advances in technology are crucial keys to the development of the superior culture of the twenty-third and twenty-fourth centuries. Yet technology is not understood as essentially good in and of itself. The Borg, for instance, have superior technology to that of the Federation and deploy technology for purposes that seem evil from the Starfleet perspective. But in many episodes the technology of the *Enterprise* and others produces miracles that save the day. Planets are delivered from the threat of destruction, enemies are annihilated, and even the dead are brought back to life. So the same tools used for destructive purposes by miscreants are used for constructive purposes by our heroes. In Star Trek, then, technology is morally neutral. Its relationship to morality is fluid, based in the intentionality of the user rather than in the technology itself. As to the moral force of any technological innovation, the Star Trek position seems to be, Who can say how things will turn out?

Evil Twins

There is another theme in Star Trek that runs counter to this Taoist-style trend we have been discussing; it has far greater affinity with the Zoroastrian view of good and evil. This is the frequent theme of the evil twin. This theme twists the plots through the appearance of alter egos, actual "twins" (e.g., Data and Lore), and alternative universes. In each situation good and evil are opposed in alternative versions of the same character(s). This theme is a mainstay for Star Trek writers. The first example from the Original Series, "The Enemy Within," was broadcast in October 1966; "alternative universe" episodes were going strong in the final year of *Deep Space Nine* some thirty years later.

In "The Enemy Within" Kirk is beamed up to the *Enterprise* in two identical forms when a transporter malfunctions. One is evil, the other good. Apparently the technical glitch has divided Kirk's mind along Zoroastrian ethical lines while duplicating his body. The evil Kirk is immediately up to no good while the good Kirk wallows in second-guessing himself (Kirk's boldness of character apparently belongs to his dark side). Eventually all this is sorted out without too much damage being done. Yeoman Rand defends her honor from Kirk's dark side tooth and nail—literally! Scotty and Spock then arrange the technological wizardry necessary to recombine the Kirks.

"The Alternative Factor" (March 1967) returned to the alter-ego theme during that first season. In this episode, a magnetic anomaly leads Kirk to a strange planet where the only human who dwells there claims he is battling a horrible criminal who has destroyed his civilization. As the plot develops, it appears that the man is trapped between parallel universes and that the criminal is his alter ego. The episode ends with this strange man, whose name is Lazarus, isolated and trapped in this battle with himself for all eternity.

Both episodes undergird popular notions of cosmic good and evil—for instance, the guardian angels and devils that stand on our shoulders, pulling us one way or the other. Some might say "the devil made me do it!" But in "The Enemy Within" the anti-Kirk is unstable physically as well as morally, and had the crew not been able to rejoin the twins, we might have been left with only the good Kirk (which certainly would have doomed the series, since the good Kirk is an ineffectual twit).

"Mirror, Mirror" (Original Series, October 1967) develops the notion of the alternative universe. Here, an ion storm causes Kirk, McCoy, Scotty, and Uhura to be transported to a parallel universe in which evil and good are reversed. Rather than the Federation, the anti-*Enterprise* represents an evil empire in which discipline is enforced by torture and promotion usually occurs through assassination. As the good officers are transported to the anti-*Enterprise*, the evil imperial Kirk, McCoy, Scotty, and Uhura arrive in this universe. After various adventures both parties are returned to their respective universes and starships. There are other examples of alternative universes (see esp. *Deep Space Nine*, "The Emperor's New Cloak"), but in order to fully understand the good-versus-evil dichotomy in Star Trek we must consider the most celebrated evil twin of all: Lore, Data's elder brother in *Star Trek: The Next Generation.*

Lore debuts in the first-season episode "Datalore," in which he is discovered disassembled on Omicron Theta, the planet where Noonien Soong created Data. When the android is assembled by *Enterprise* scientists, he is an exact replica of Data—but with an essential difference: Lore lacks Data's sense of morality. Of course, that's not the way Lore sees the situation; from his perspective it is Data who is the imperfect replica of the perfect Lore. Indeed, the inhabitants of Omicron Theta were so fearful of Lore that Soong deactivated the android. But Lore had already orchestrated his revenge on his enemies. He had lured the Crystalline Entity to the planet. This interstellar traveler nourished itself on the life-energy of other beings. When it reached a planet inhabited by life-forms, it absorbed all their energy, wreaking complete destruction on the planet and leaving behind lifeless material. This was the fate of the colony on Omicron Theta. Lore "survived" (as he had planned) because, being deactivated, he was not "alive" when the Crystalline Entity arrived.

Lore is the epitome of selfish brilliance. He has all the superhuman powers of Data but none of the modesty or self-control. He reappears in several episodes, finally being destroyed after taking control of a renegade group of Borg. Lore is an interesting character who gives the gifted actor Brent Spiner a role to display his talents. The android is devoid of any of the softer, humanistic virtues and thus may stand as a good example of pure evil. He even has a grudge against Terrans, due to the fact that he was dismantled by the Terran colonists of his home planet. Lore has the potential to be a holy terror, but in fact his ability to wreak havoc is limited, as his enemies are onto his tricks. Data, who sees in Lore a genuinely kindred spirit and who, at times, is even in league with his brother, finally realizes that he has no choice but to terminate him.

In Lore we come closest to a Catholic dogma that evil is a privation—an absence—of good. This view holds that good is the default moral quality of the universe as created by God and that evil is created when someone chooses to turn away from God's good plan, like Adam and Eve. Good thus always comes first; evil is never equal to good on the cosmic scale, always lesser. Lore lacks the discernment to see that evil is inferior because it is not part of his software. He would have to be reprogrammed to see the charm of goodness, but Data has the requisite programming.

Have we found Cosmic Evil in Lore? Not really. Even though there is no good in Lore, he nevertheless is a human creation, not a part of any cosmic order. In a sense, his case evokes the sense of metaphysical evil—flawed design—rather than cosmic evil. He's a cyber version of a criminal with a deprived childhood—hardly a Prince of Darkness. Among the many villains in Star Trek, Lore is rather minor in the big scheme of things. He is an interesting foil to Data and plays against his brother's quest for humanity. As a force of evil, however, as a cosmic opposition to good, Lore falls a few circuits short.

Assimilate This!

And the Borg Collective? Given its policy of complete assimilation, it represents the enemy of all species in the galaxies. But even though it seems to represent the dark side of technology, it is by no means an agent of any cosmic evil. Our first hints of the Borg come in the form of planetary genocide, the utter destruction of civilizations. We learn that they are a composite race that exists by assimilating individuals, species, technology, raw materials—anything and everything. That is scary enough, but when we learn that their technology is superior to that of the Federation and its allies, well, all hell breaks loose. The Borg are also good at what they do, assimilating even Picard (who becomes Locutus, their spokesman to the Federation) and attacking Sector 001 in the Alpha Quadrant (that is, the Earth).

The Borg are a powerful image for technology gone mad, but they possess a human face. They are cyborgs, or technologically enhanced humans (humanoids, to be exact). Thus, they are more like us than the unemotional HAL, the haywire computer of *2001: A Space Odyssey,* who was humanlike in his death. They are also more like us than even the cyborgs of the *Terminator* film series, as all of the Borg seem to be enhanced humanoids, not the manufactured cyborgs of *Terminator.* The Borg are assimilated biological life-forms, not techno-creations that affect human features. The fear factor is thus fundamental: *This could happen to you.*

The Borg Queen, played so convincingly by Alice Krige in *Star Trek: First Contact,* allows us to personify the Borg in a central agent, although many fans found that move disappointing. Many saw the Borg as more convincing as a collective without a leader than as an ant colony mindlessly devoted to its queen. In *First Contact,* however, the Queen *is* the Borg Collective, and she has all the morality of Lore. She's completely self-absorbed, and she's high-maintenance.

This amoral self-absorption is, perhaps, the best candidate for the Star Trek definition of evil. The members of Starfleet are dedicated to service and, as Spock declares as he dies in *Star Trek II: The Wrath of Khan,* "the needs of the many outweigh the needs of the few, or one." Kirk's corollary to this surfaces in *Star Trek III: The Search for Spock,* actually confirming the sentiment rather than contradicting it: As with Dumas's classic three musketeers, the overall motto is "one for all and all for one." The Borg Queen, in contrast, has no qualms about sacrificing scads of Borg drones to save herself. Her sardonic twist is that she *is* the collective—for her the rallying cry is "all for one." Her own self-sacrifice for the greater good is not on her agenda.

Thus, the Borg Collective is a perfect enemy—the alter ego of the Federation and its allies, an evil twin on a grand scale. Whereas the Federation and its allies stand for individual freedom and the self-determination of species and individuals, the Borg stand for the assimilation of all individuality—personal, cultural, species-based—into a single whole. It represents the violent denial of all that the Federation and its allies hold to be good. Assimilated individuals become drones, automatons selflessly carrying out the needs of the collective in a distorted mockery of the altruistic selflessness of the Federation ideal. Once assimilated, there is virtually no way to return.

Picard, who survived assimilation and return, fully believes that it is kinder to kill comrades who are assimilated than to let them survive as Borg drones. But the Borg drones don't swallow the Federation line. They add the distinctiveness of assimilated races to the Borg Collective in the quest for perfection. As Locutus puts it in the *Deep Space Nine* episode "Emissary," the Borg aim is "to raise the quality of life for all species." Thus, the Borg ideal, although repellent to the Federation, nevertheless has logic.

In *Next Generation*, the episode "I, Borg" explores the humanity of Borg drones in a way that portrays the repellent nature of the Borg Collective. A young male Borg is captured by the *Enterprise* and is studied while on board. Initially, the plan is to infect him with a computer virus as a means of destroying the Collective, but the plan is dropped as inhumane. This Borg, given the human name Hugh, becomes an appealing character. His inborn human potential of individuality is sparked through friendship with Geordi; still a Borg, he leaves the ship a very different person.

Even more poignant are the *Voyager* episodes that trace the reassimilation of the Borg character Seven of Nine into human culture. Clearly, Seven has no interest in leaving the Collective, which is the only existence she recalls. It is frightening for her to be cut off from the rest of her race. Whereas before she was in constant communication with the myriad voices of the collective via her cyborg implants, now she is alone. And this is terrifying for her—as terrifying as it is for humans to contemplate Borg assimilation. Without the voices of the Collective constantly passing through her mind, keeping her in unbroken contact with the other members of her race, Seven is lost. She can't bear to be alone, has never been alone (actually an individual child before assimilation, she has repressed the memories of her trauma). As far as she can recall, her only purpose in life—her very identity—is found through interconnection in the Borg Collective. With it, she knows who she is and what she is to do: Life has meaning, the galaxy is being improved. Without the link, she is nothing, a mere individual, a cipher in an empty universe. Our notions of individuality have no charm whatsoever for Seven. What can be the point of being completely isolated from all other beings? How can that possibly be good?

These Borg examples undergird a central value in Star Trek, that is, the humanistic value that promotes understanding of otherness as a means to overcoming evil. Are the Borg a threat to human existence? To be sure they are: Evil is not always just a psychological projection. The Borg have to be stopped, but that doesn't mean that they have to be demonized. We have more than one tool to use in dealing with their lot. Violent force is necessary, since the Borg would appreciate the moral force of pacifism about as much as would the Nazis. But along with force, we can use understanding. "I, Borg" shows that even for Jean-Luc Picard, who has deeply personal reasons to hate and fear the Borg Collective, genocide is not an option. That goes too far. But they have another weapon, an uncertain one, in Hugh. And it does work: Hugh becomes an unwitting mole; he and his Borg unit become infected with the individuality meme and cease to function as a collective unit. Unfortunately these particular drones become dominated by Lore in the *Next Generation* episodes "Descent, Parts I and II," but with the help of the *Enterprise* crew, and Hugh's sense of loyalty to his comrades, they survive as individuals.

In *Voyager*, the introduction of Seven of Nine develops themes of Federation people working with Borg drones in collaborative ventures. This, of course, takes place far from the Alpha Quadrant and begins with drones isolated from the link, but nevertheless there is collaboration. In "Unity," an episode first aired in winter 1997, an injured Commander Chakotay is healed of serious injuries by linking to a local, limited "Collective Consciousness" that the isolated drones have been able to construct. As the drones are able to establish this planet-specific link for their local Collective, the clear principle is established: There are some positive aspects to Borg assimilation, particularly superior healing techniques and a means to establish and maintain unity and harmony among peoples.

This is a remarkable development, but there is more. In the season finale, "Scorpion," a two-part episode, Janeway finds it necessary to make a treaty with the Borg. It is a very limited one and occurs because of dire circumstances that threaten the existence of the Collective as well as *Voyager*, but the deal is made. Nothing changes the fact that, as with the Klingon Empire, the Borg Collective can be "humanized." Once more, an excellent enemy faces the disaster of being made into a friend.

Final Move: Prophets and Pah-wraiths

So far, we've been arguing that the imaginal universe of Star Trek is one in which good and evil are relative, rather than absolute, qualities. That is, they are matters of interpretation, differing from culture to culture and from situation to situation rather than inhering in aspects of the universe itself. There is no Wise Lord or benevolent God who created and rules the Star Trek universe, no Evil One to provide cosmic opposition. However, events that unfold in the last two seasons of *Deep Space Nine* directly challenge this thesis. The challenge comes not in the Founders—the powerful race of shapeshifters to which Deep Space Nine's security chief, Odo, belongs—who make war on the Federation and its allies. Rather, the alteration comes in aspects of the Bajoran religion that are revealed clearly only in seasons six and seven of *Deep Space Nine*.[2]

The key are the Pah-wraiths, who debuted during season five in "The Assignment." Keiko O'Brien returns from a visit to Bajor with a new personality. She is possessed, and the possessing entity forces her husband, Miles, to alter the station deflector in order to send a lethal beam into the Wormhole. Here, as in other episodes, we have a nasty possessor who is willing to injure Keiko in order to persuade Miles to do its bidding. It is a Pah-wraith, a member of a class of beings in Bajoran mythology who serve as the demonic spiritual enemies of the Prophets. The Pah-wraith who possesses Keiko wants to destroy the Prophets with the deflector beam that Miles O'Brien is modifying. The beam destroys the Pah-wraith instead, freeing Keiko in a scientific exorcism. But now we know that there are evil spirits in Bajoran religion who are opposed to the good Prophets, that is, there are evil demons and good gods.

Deep Space Nine presents the Pah-wraiths as parallels to Christian understanding of Satan and his league. The only named Pah-wraith is Kosst Amojan, who apparently was banished from the Celestial Temple of the Prophets (i.e., the Bajoran Wormhole) and seeks revenge. His aim is to destroy the Prophets and free his associates from their imprisonment in the Fire Caves on Bajor in order, apparently, to control the universe. Like the Prophets (and in a manner that echoes many Terran mythologies), the Pah-wraiths use human intermediaries to achieve their goals.

Keiko's possession allows us to make specific references to earthly religions, especially Christianity. Any reader of the Gospels of the New Testament is well familiar with the miracles of Jesus. Prominent among them are exorcisms of demons from human beings. Most of the time the reasons for the possession are obscure; it seems that humans are simply comfortable abodes for demons. But these demons are generally understood to be in league with Satan, who tries unsuccessfully to subvert Jesus' mission by tempting him with earthly glory. But there is a case of possession in which Satan's plan reflects that of the Pah-wraith: to destroy the good by human interference. The Gospels of Luke and John state that the betrayal of Jesus by Judas is preceded by a possession: "Then Satan *entered into* Judas called Iscariot, who was one of the twelve; he went away and conferred with the chief priests and officers of the temple police about how he might betray him [Jesus] to them" (Luke 22:3–4; cf. John 13:26–27; emphasis added). Jesus knows that he will be betrayed and identifies Judas as the betrayer. Were these modern writers, we would understand the description metaphorically, but ancient writers lived in a world where people routinely believed in the reality of demonic possession. In some of the Gospels, then, Satan uses Judas as a means to accomplish the death of Jesus. He does this by entering into him and causing him to do evil. Once the act is accomplished, Judas is remorseful and commits suicide (according to both Matthew and Acts). The parallel between these possessions for the purpose of accomplishing cosmic evil is crystal-clear.

Late in season six the Pah-wraiths return to the station in "The Reckoning." Again we see the possession theme, along with another Christian idea: a final cosmic battle between Good and Evil that, according to prophecy, will usher in a new age, a golden age of peace and happiness for Bajor. It is Kai Winn who provides this information. Played by Louise Fletcher, this Kai is a regular minor character, the supreme religious leader on Bajor, ambitious for power and rather weak in faith. Here, Kira and Jake Sisko (the Emissary's son) are possessed, by a Prophet and Kosst Amojan (the evil Pah-wraith) respectively, and they battle for control of the future of the universe on the station promenade deck with lethal beams of light. But before the outcome is decided, Kai Winn releases a radiation field from the station that disrupts and ends the possessions. Sisko knew of but had refused to use the energy source, trusting in the Prophets to decide the outcome of the duel. Winn's faith in the Prophets was weaker (indeed, both Sisko and Kira are specifically contrasted with Winn on the issue of faith). Winn is interested in personal status and jealous of those whom the Prophets call to service. Although there are differences between Sisko's developing and Kira's abiding faith in the Prophets, the contrast with Winn's use of faith as a tool for personal advancement is clear.

The other important player in this narrative thread is Gul Dukat, the Cardassian who had overseen the occupation of Bajor. Dukat, too, is ambitious, but he adds to that a real talent for brutality and treachery. Played with élan by Marc Alaimo, Dukat has some appealing qualities, but they are overshadowed by his dark side. Since the time that his daughter was murdered by one of his former lieutenants because of her Bajoran sympathies, Dukat has been mentally unbalanced. In the final season of *Deep Space Nine*, he has by no means entirely regained his sanity; he seems rather obsessive but is otherwise outwardly functional. In "Tears of the Prophets," the season-six finale, he is in league with the Pah-wraiths and becomes possessed by one of them (apparently the ubiquitous Kosst Amojan, who seems to have been released from a Bajoran statue. Dukat is transported to Deep Space Nine, where he kills Jadzia Dax (the symbiont survives to inhabit Ezri) and destroys the orb of the Prophets that allows Bajorans to receive visions. This closes the Wormhole and alters the relationship of the Prophets to Bajor and to Sisko the Emissary. This will not be the last time Dukat is possessed. Surgically altered to appear as a Bajoran rather than a Cardassian, he goes on to assume the leadership of a heretical, cultlike Bajoran religious group that worships the Pah-wraiths—a twist on Christian obsessions about Satan-worshipers—and leads them to a mass-suicide ritual. Kira foils the plot, but Dukat escapes again.

The Pah-wraith cult had already been presented, through the medium of an assassin who tries to kill Sisko. They, however, are not central to the plot-line. Dukat is, and he appears on Bajor in order to befriend Kai Winn and subvert her. He does this treacherously, feigning love for the aging Kai while undermining her faith in the Prophets. The fact that Winn receives a vision that the Prophets will provide her with the Guide makes Dukat seem to be literally heaven-sent. Dukat seems to be both the agent of the Pah-wraiths and the Guide the Prophets have apparently foretold. It is more likely, however, that Winn's vision is a false one sent by the Pah-wraiths to delude her. Nevertheless, Winn and Dukat will go on to fulfill the plan of the Prophets.

Winn trusts Dukat little, and she leads him to the Fire Caves of Bajor, where the Pah-wraiths were imprisoned by the Prophets millennia ago. Bringing the forbidden book of the Kosst Amojan, which contains the secret ritual spells that will free the Pah-wraiths, they reach the central cave, which is anything but fiery. When Dukat mentions his disappointment, Winn reads a few words from the book, and the pit into which they are gazing becomes filled with flame. Fiery wisps leaping in the inferno are clearly the wraiths themselves, still imprisoned but now active and visible. Joyously, Winn flings her religious garments (but not *all* her clothes) into the flames, saying, "I rid myself of the Prophets and shed a lifetime of hypocrisy." She dedicates herself to the Pah-wraiths, feeling like a young girl awaiting her first lover.

Apparently still in the spirit of giving, Winn then offers Dukat a celebratory cup of wine. But it is poisoned, and Dukat, as he feels himself dying, is told that he is to be a sacrifice to the Pah-wraiths: "Someone worthy of them," Winn says. "Who better than you?" The sacrifice releases the wraiths. Winn, who expects that the Pah-wraiths will enter into her body and possess her, is stunned into unconsciousness. But then the Pah-wraiths (or perhaps only Kosst Amojan) enter Dukat's body, animating not Winn, as she expected, but him. Dukat is returned to his Cardassian form, although with the red eyes of Hollywood demonology. He, not Winn, is the chosen vessel of the Pah-wraiths.

Meanwhile, back at the station, Sisko is at a party celebrating the victorious end of the war between the Dominion and the Federation. Suddenly, he realizes the meaning of it all: "I understand now, what I have to do. What I was meant to do." He takes a shuttle and speeds to the surface.

In the cave, the possessed Dukat is expounding to Winn the future, now that the Pah-wraiths are about to be finally freed: "Soon, the Pah-wraiths will burn across Bajor, the Celestial Temple [the Wormhole], the Alpha Quadrant. Can you picture it? An *entire universe* set in flames to burn for all eternity" (emphasis added). Sisko arrives, but Dukat is aware of it before the emissary appears, saying, "The Prophets have sent me a gift, their beloved emissary sent forth like an avenging angel to slay the demon." "I should have known the demon would be you," Sisko replies. But Sisko is powerless against Dukat's infernal powers, until Kai Winn intervenes by raising the book in order to throw it into the rising flames. Then, in an instant, Dukat transfers the book to his own hands, Winn is engulfed in flames by the Pah-wraiths, and Sisko leaps up and charges Dukat, hurling both of them into the fiery pit. As they fall, Sisko releases Dukat, who, along with the book, disappears into the flames.

What does this represent? An angel sent by the Prophets who battles a possessing demon representing the Pah-wraiths. This is, of course, a symbolic representation: Both are really humanoid agents inspired or possessed by the deities. Also, we see a fiery pit inhabited by demonic beings and hear of a cosmic battle, foretold as "The Reckoning," between good and evil (championed by Sisko and Dukat, respectively), with the stakes being not Bajor and its religion but the entire universe. This is a stunning parallel to what many Christians understand as being foretold in prophetic scriptures such as Revelation. Just so, the whole *Deep Space Nine* business is foretold by the Prophets, who revealed the Reckoning and the possibility of the golden age to follow, imprisoned the Pah-wraiths in the first place, and, indeed sent their Emissary (Sisko) to accomplish the final, eternal imprisonment of the Pah-wraiths and, for good measure, their agent, Dukat. How do we know this? It's revealed to Sisko, who does not die and is immediately transported from the flaming pit to the Celestial Temple. There he meets not the Father but his Mother, the Sarah Prophet, who remarks, "The Emissary has completed his task."

Sisko: But the Pah-wraiths?
Sarah: You have returned them to their prison within the Fire Caves.
Sisko: The book was the key, wasn't it?
Sarah: It's a door that can never be opened again.
Sisko: And Dukat, is he dead?
Sarah: Dukat is with the Pah-wraiths. Your time of trial has ended. You need to rest now. You're with us now.

Note that Sisko sacrificed himself to destroy Dukat and the book. He fell headlong into the flames with every expectation of being burned to death. But it was worth it to save the universe and, of course, fulfill his destiny. The Prophets intervene just at the right moment (their sense of timing perfect) and bring him to their own realm. In a manner that parallels hero stories the world over (as well as the death and rebirth of Spock), particularly the narrative of Jesus Christ, Sisko sacrifices himself for everyone's salvation, goes willingly to a horrible death, and is saved by divine intervention and transported bodily to a heavenly realm where he has much to learn. There's even a postresurrection appearance that is quite in line with canonical descriptions of Jesus that emphasize women as the first witnesses to his resurrection. It's Kasidy Yates (Mrs. Sisko), who has a vision of the Celestial Temple in which she and Ben embrace. Then he tells her of his necessary sojourn there but promises that he will return: "Maybe a year, maybe yesterday, but I will be back." This recalls what the Gospel of Mark says about the timing of the return of Christ: "But about that day or hour no one knows, neither the angels in heaven, nor the Son, but only the Father" (13:32).[3] Sisko, like Jesus, was foreordained to do these things. As is typical of mythological heroes, his birth was extraordinary; he is no ordinary human, although he appears to be such. He is now with the Celestial beings, and we don't know what he will bring when he returns.

This cosmology is directly based on the Zoroastrian ethical dualism, especially as it is found in Christianity. The Prophets have an eternal plan to destroy the infernal Pah-wraiths once and for all, and the human being Sisko is created as a central part of that plan. He is to become the Emissary, the *Deep Space Nine* analog of the Christian messiah. Cosmic good and evil battle through the medium of humanoid agents: first Kira and Jake, then Winn, Dukat, and Sisko. In the Christian story, according to God's plan Jesus is created as a man sent by God to destroy the infernal power of sin and thus save all humanity. His enemies, inspired by Satan, are all too human. The cosmic battle is finally played out on a time-bound, human scale, and good wins.

There are crucial differences between the stories, but the parallels are striking. After three decades, the Western default narrative has finally taken hold of the Star Trek universe. Regardless of the writers' intent, the development correlated with the rise of interest in religion in the United States in the 1990s. And Gene Roddenberry's death in 1991 may well have diminished the influence of his secular humanist viewpoint. But do the events of the final season of *Deep Space Nine* shatter the fundamental view of Evil in the Star Trek universe? Has the Christian world view supplanted humanism?

One could make the case that this is yet another alien religion and that Star Trek's basic attitude toward evil remains unchanged. On the one hand, the Prophets are Bajoran gods; on the other they are the Wormhole Aliens, and thus are a species. As such they are more like the Q Continuum than biological humanoids, but they are life-forms subject to the laws of physics. This interpretation relegates both the Wormhole Aliens and the Pah-wraiths to a scientific as opposed to a supernatural realm of explanation. They can be manipulated and even destroyed by scientific technology, as in "The Assignment" and "The Reckoning." This interpretation, then, would claim that the Federation occupation of Deep Space Nine has simply put Sisko and the others in the middle of a local war between weird aliens understood by the Bajorans as gods and demons. Evil is thus relativized and limited to the cultural understandings of the Bajorans.[4]

This interpretation does not hold, overwhelmed as it is by Western religious themes in the series as a whole. Note also that the premier episode of *Deep Space Nine* ("Emissary, Parts 1 and 2") introduces Bajoran religious concepts and that the process of coming to terms with this local religious role is critical to the development of Sisko's character throughout the series, as is the development of the Prophets and Bajoran religion. Sisko's struggles against his Bajoran role as Emissary, particularly when they conflict with his Starfleet duties, are an important issue. Finally, in an acquiescence that viewers might associate with the onset of faith, he accepts this religious role as the essential part of his identity. The values of Bajoran religion permeate the central story line of the entire *Deep Space Nine* series.

The portrayal of religious faith in *Deep Space Nine* is interesting as well. Although Worf is noteworthy for his religious adherence, and the Ferengi have religious aspects to their capitalism, it is Kira Nerys who is most frequently portrayed in terms of her faith in her religion, former Bajoran freedom fighter though she may be. Indeed, her faith was a key to her persistence as a member of the Bajoran underground during the Cardassian occupation. Although this faith may occasionally be shown to be problematic, nowhere is its essential validity for her questioned. The fact that the writers emphasize faith as an essential aspect of Bajoran religion is also noteworthy, as it reflects the values of Christianity and the other Western religions of Judaism and Islam. Here, too, as many have noticed, Christian values are in the fore. The writers also exploit Christianity-based models of true faith and false faith by contrasting the attitudes of Kira and Kai Winn, among others.

But there are essential differences between what is going on in *Deep Space Nine* and Christianity. First of all, we must point out that, fundamental though it may be to American attitudes, the centrality of faith is not a universal phenomenon in human religions, many of which are more interested in how people actually live their lives than in what they profess to believe. Furthermore, Kira's faith is in beings whose existence is validated by her own direct experience (her possession by a Prophet in "The Reckoning"), by the direct experience of her friend and commander, Benjamin Sisko, and, in traditional Star Trek fashion, by scientific investigation as well. The reality of the Prophets is unquestioned. No character in the *Deep Space Nine* series doubts the existence of the Wormhole Aliens or of the Pah-wraiths. They may, as does O'Brien in "Children of Time," doubt the tenets of Bajoran religion (e.g., that the Prophets arrange our lives for the best and that we must be fatalistic), but the very existence of the Prophets is beyond doubt. Thus the location of faith in Bajoran religion is not at all the same as the location of faith in Christianity in the West since the scientific revolution.

Nevertheless, by the end of *Deep Space Nine* we seem to find ourselves in a different universe compared to *Next Generation*. Here, the local Bajoran religion has values that are literally universal. Sisko's religious role as Emissary is as central to the series as it is to his character, and we learn in the end that it began before Sisko's birth on Earth. How much of the other events in *Deep Space Nine* should we understand as being caused by the cosmic plan of the Prophets? The occupation of Bajor by the Cardassians? That is, of course, the situation that brought Gul Dukat to the area in the first place. If the Prophets could cause Sisko to be born, why couldn't they arrange the occupation of Bajor? The war between the Federation and the Founders? The Wormhole, the dwelling place of the Prophets, is of course the connection between the two combatants. Did the Prophets arrange the war? The Pah-wraith-possessed Dukat's remarks in the final episode clearly talk of a universal conflagration, hardly an eschatology limited to Bajor. Much remains unclear. In any case, it is indisputable that these religious issues, derived for the most part from popular culture versions of Christianity, are an essential narrative and thematic core of the series. It seems that these developments have finally aligned the universe of Star Trek with the ethical dualism of Star Wars and the Western tradition in general. This is a far cry from the secular humanist vision of Gene Roddenberry, and it is no accident that these episodes were developed well after the death of Star Trek's inspirational founder. Although we are not able to account for the reasons motivating the creators at Paramount, it is clear that the final season of *Deep Space Nine* fundamentally alters the view of evil in the Star Trek universe.

As for the future, who can say how things will turn out?

3

Shamans, Prophets, Priests, and Mystics: Star Trek's Religious Specialists

SUSAN L. SCHWARTZ

In the most recent film in the Star Trek series, *Star Trek: Insurrection*, Captain Jean-Luc Picard of Starship *Enterprise* falls for a woman named Anij, one of the Ba'ku race of humanoids located on an isolated planet surrounded by magical rings. The planet is located in a peculiar part of space called the "Briar Patch" by the Federation. As the plot unfolds, it becomes clear that the Ba'ku have achieved what is, perhaps, the ultimate human goal: immortality and perpetual youth. Anij is more than three hundred years old thanks to the "metaphasic radiation" generated by the rings around the planet. Having rejected technology and embraced a pastoral, isolated, peaceful, and idyllic existence, the Ba'ku have discovered how to focus their thoughts to achieve extraordinary effects. In the words of the empath Deanna Troi, the ship's counselor, they have "incredible mental discipline." Their planet is "a sanctuary of life." It is Shangri-la.

The threat in this story comes from the Son'a race, technological wizards who have used their scientific skills to keep themselves alive by artificial means: genetic manipulation. Obsessed by age and appearance, they stretch their skin in a gruesome procedure, a parody of the Hollywood face-lift. Their bodies produce toxins that no longer can be neutralized; they are dying, putrefying. Their mental state can only be described as obsessive-compulsive; they have become decadent, ruthless, loveless—ugly in every sense. The Son'a are the opposite of the Ba'ku in every way. And they intend to steal immortality from the Ba'ku by means of an elaborate scheme, backed by Starfleet itself. The fact that the Son'a turn out to be exiled Ba'ku makes a perfect irony—and a perfect circle.

Insurrection presents the Federation as torn by the demands of time and space, unsure of its own principles, and willing to seek alliances with dubious characters like the Son'a in order to offset losses to enemies like the Dominion and the Borg. We see Picard and his crew frustrated by the need to direct their efforts to diplomatic duties: "Can anyone remember when we used to be explorers?" Picard's rhetorical question suggests that life in the twenty-fourth century for these characters feels a lot like life in modern America. Harried, pressured, unsure of our purpose and the point of all our frantic activity, we long—or think we long—for a slower pace, for time to think about what is really important. When Anij tells Picard that if he stayed with them he would stop asking questions, "stop reviewing what happened yesterday, stop planning for tomorrow," it sounds incredibly attractive to him—and to us. The planet itself looks like Paradise; its isolation seems ideal. When it turns out that along with eternal youth, peace, and beauty the Ba'ku have also achieved mental clarity and the ability to control their perception of time, to turn inward the power that Western cultures have traditionally turned outward, the seduction is complete. As Anij puts it: "You explore the universe. We've discovered that a single moment in time can be a universe in itself, full of powerful forces." The fact that the line is delivered by an attractive, intelligent, secure woman completes the effect. The scenario is reminiscent of the West's fascination with Tibetan Buddhism at the end of the second millennium.

Anij demonstrates her powers to Picard, but she will not answer him when he asks how she does it. As time slows, we see water flowing in slow motion and a hummingbird's wings beating as it hovers. "It took us hundreds of years to learn it doesn't have to take hundreds of years to learn," she says, and indeed by film's end Picard is able to slow time to save her life. Like the Tibetan Buddhism of our imagination, these highly specialized skills need only to be learned; they are in principle available to all. With a skilled and willing teacher, a conducive atmosphere, and the appropriate state of mind, anything is possible.

But who, and what, is Anij? Without mentioning religion once, *Insurrection* gives us a model of a religious specialist. Such a person is able to induce an altered state of awareness in which the appreciation of life is transformed. She might also have the ability actually to manipulate time, space, and physical reality, and to act as a teacher or transmitter of a different (and superior) reality. Anij performs all of these functions, and she manages to make it sexy, too!

Star Trek in its many incarnations has often introduced us to such characters. Q certainly qualifies, as does the Traveler; there are many others. They are women and men, old, young, or ageless, unconstrained by normal bounds of time and space. They work their effects for good or ill, and it is often impossible to guess their motives or purpose. Their abilities and qualities are familiar from religious traditions of Earth, where such persons are known to us as shamans, sorcerers, prophets, and mystics. Sometimes they mediate between another force or larger reality and the human realm, or between physical and psychological understandings of reality. They are often *enablers*, opening doors of perception and understanding. But they may also cause big trouble, and they can be extremely dangerous.

The academic study of religion recognizes different types of specialists and makes useful distinctions among them. There's a gray area that bears watching, however, as we assign titles to such figures. For example, a shaman performs a healing function in traditional cultures, a priest other, often more formal ritual ceremonies. Yet either may practice a form of sacrifice and preside over ritual functions. A prophet can have a special form of vision and an authoritative voice to make predictions and prognostications, whereas a mystic is a more solitary practitioner, someone who lives apart from the community and only rarely interacts with others. Yet both seek a personal and intense relationship with a spiritual source of power. Fixed and narrow guidelines thus obscure the fact that many categories overlap, and insisting upon distinctions for the sake of differentiation can ultimately be misleading. Not surprisingly, Star Trek is not overly concerned with the finer points of such definitions. These problems are not a central issue in this chapter, but they should be kept in mind.

Star Trek places and characterizes religious specialists in the series to serve many different purposes. Sometimes they are potentially dangerous charlatans like Ardra; sometimes they are deluded madmen like Sybok. Alternatively, religious specialists may serve as powerful agents of spiritual and physical transformation, as Anij does in *Insurrection*. In short, we see the appearance and activity of such characters in Star Trek treated with *ambivalence*, which is also the way they have been treated by most cultures in human history.

It might finally be argued that Star Trek, despite a sort of "creed" endorsing the supremacy of science and rationality, has decided that religious specialists have a genuine and important role to play, for good or ill, in its universe. Echoing contemporary Western culture, Star Trek has a fascination with powers beyond technology. The claim that unique individuals with particular insight and ability derive "higher powers" from a mysterious and powerful "otherworldly source" is no less a topic of concern in the Star Trek future than it is in our world. What is it that convinces perfectly "ordinary" people to follow a teacher or preacher despite hardship, sacrifice, and ridicule? Is this a human weakness or a human strength? On what basis are we to decide whether such a person is legitimate, the cause just and true, or the results worthwhile and inspired? Star Trek cannot answer these questions. It is, after all, offering a *representation* of these figures filtered through the lens of popular culture, not engaging in scholarly discourse. Neither is Star Trek neutral on this topic, for given its skeptical approach to religion in general, it is more often the case that its charismatic religious characters are portrayed as imitations and fakes. It is notable, therefore, that in the cases presented below the writers and producers seem willing to entertain the possibility that under certain circumstances religious specialists might be viable, that they might have real ability, authority, and identity. Through example, Star Trek can show us ways in which religious specialists act, succeed or fail, leave a wake of mystery to ponder. In the end, the creators and writers involved with developing these stories clearly want to leave the possibility open.

Bajor: Beyond the Belly of the Beast

The most obvious examples of religious specialists considered to be "genuine" by Star Trek standards occur in the *Deep Space Nine* series. In the very first episode, appropriately entitled "Emissary," we are amazed to find that the Starfleet captain, Benjamin Sisko, is expected by the religious leader of the planet Bajor, Kai Opaka, to serve a religious function. He is a reluctant choice. He does not even want this assignment, on an abandoned wreck of a space station positioned near a wreck of a planet; much less does he want to be considered some religious prophet. Like the biblical Jonah, who was swallowed by a whale in his attempt to avoid God's will that he serve as a prophet, Sisko seems an unlikely candidate for the role. The first words spoken to him by a Bajoran upon his arrival are "the Prophets await you." At first he avoids the invitation, but he becomes increasingly intrigued by Bajoran religion after meeting Kira, the Bajoran major assigned to his station, and learning that it is from their religious beliefs that the surface dwellers draw their strength and unity.

He is summoned by their religious leader, Kai Opaka, who "rarely sees anyone" and travels to a religious structure that resembles a monastery or ashram.[1] He is mystified by her expectations, and it is only through experience of the mysterious orb—one of nine artifacts called by the Bajorans a "tear of the Prophets"—that he begins to suspect there may be something going on here with some basis in a reality he can recognize. For he is a tortured soul, and both the Kai and the orb recognize his suffering immediately. And then he, like Jonah, is swallowed, not by a whale but by its cosmic equivalent: a wormhole. On an exploratory mission, he is "taken" to the Celestial Temple, as it is known on Bajor. There he is questioned by those the Bajorans consider to be the Prophets (the Wormhole Aliens to Starfleet). Not only have they served as the religious basis for Bajoran life; they constructed the Wormhole itself. Their reach extends considerably farther, as it turns out. Throughout the course of the series, Sisko not only accepts the fact that he has been chosen by the Bajoran Prophets to establish their primacy but also comes to recognize that this is his true calling, his true identity, his destiny. He is there to provide, even to *be*, the means by which the will of the Prophets is realized. He is the "Emissary" of the episode's title, a word that brings to mind associations with a messenger (the Greek equivalent is *angelos*, hence "angel").[2]

Several episodes offer visions experienced by Sisko, Kira Narys, and other Bajoran characters as a result of contact with these objects. The problem with such experiences, as we know from Terran religion, is how to interpret them. Many episodes focus on the humanoid tendency to misinterpret divine messages under the influence of desire, ambition, political expediency, and even darker impulses such as revenge, hatred, and immorality. Interestingly, those who serve as the Kai are not immune from such misguided impulses; one could read such examples as Star Trek's critique of clergy generally. The case of Kai Opaka offers yet another scenario, however.

In the episode "Battle Lines," at the end of the first season, the much-beloved Kai Opaka arrives suddenly on Deep Space Nine requesting a trip through the Wormhole. She is acting on instructions from the Prophets that she herself does not yet understand. The honor and devotion she is accorded by Kira reflect the role she has played in helping the Bajorans survive the Cardassian occupation. What she, and we, cannot know is that with the retreat of their enemy the Bajorans are poised on a new phase of their existence, and therefore a change in spiritual leadership is required. What is to become of a Kai who has outlived her purpose? The Prophets intend for her to find a new purpose elsewhere, and so she must enter the mysterious portal to emerge on the other side and crash-land on an unknown planet that has been designated a penal colony by an unknown species. Opaka dies during the incident, then is apparently resurrected. The criminals on the planet belong to two factions locked in a blood feud. For their inability to resolve their hatred they have been doomed to fight each other eternally under the surveillance of a biomechanical system, which allows them to die in pain and then restores them to life to battle again. Kai Opaka is fated to minister to them; once one has died and been restored by this system, one cannot live anywhere else.

Opaka is an acknowledged religious figure. Her abilities are acknowledged within the series as effective if mysterious. She shares a significant quality with Guinan (a *Next Generation* character discussed below). Guinan belongs to a species called El-Aurans, who "listen"; their power comes to them through their ability to hear and understand. The first Bajoran we meet on Star Trek is actually a character in the *Next Generation* series; her name is Ro Laren, and the episode is "Ensign Ro." Here and in *Deep Space Nine* we learn that the Bajorans consider one piece of jewelry essential: an elaborate earring. This is not ornamentation in the usual sense; it is religious jewelry. Bajorans believe that one's *pagh*, or "soul," is accessible through the earlobe. Bajoran religious specialists perceive the true nature of their people by holding that particular part of the anatomy, which appears to enable a telepathic transfer. Primarily oral cultures recognize that the auditory canal is a sensitive passage to the interior of a person.

In contrast, visual cultures like ours are often unaware of the power of hearing over that of vision, although our own traditions are full of references to prophets and others who instruct their followers to "hear." The Quran instructs the Islamic faithful at the outset to follow the Prophet Muhammad's example and "recite," so that what has been revealed may be heard and heeded. The iconography of Buddhism is explicit on this: The Buddha, in his many, many images, almost always has elongated earlobes. The Kai's ability to heal and transform the wounded Bajorans, as well as the embattled aliens on the penal planet, is a function of her ability to listen and know. Likewise Guinan's ability to listen and understand provides her with the opportunity to help Picard and maintain a special relationship with him over many years. These are abilities observable in many religions, enhanced and amplified in the religious specialists of alien races introduced to us on Star Trek. In the case of Sisko and Kai Opaka, we have two characters whose abilities and purpose are defined by the series using religious language and imagery. Beyond the obvious, however, are examples of religious specialists who are neither characterized nor clearly defined as such. Their roles are more ambiguous and often controversial in contemporary American culture, but this may not be the case elsewhere. As it turns out, Star Trek can imagine them quite effectively.

"He's Dead, Jim"—or Maybe Not: Who Are the Healers?

In contemporary Western cultures, the art of healing has split between those who attend to physical illnesses and those who attend to psychological/spiritual ailments, which are more difficult to define. The split between the body and the mind, or the body and the spirit, has ample precedent in Western religions and philosophies, including those popularly known as gnosticism. For most of human history, however, and in cultures other than ours, this dualism is less apparent. Currently, we have begun to suspect that curing the body without attending to the whole person is a problematic approach. Even the medical community is beginning to address what the ordinary person has long suspected: The body and the mind work, suffer, and display symptoms of distress together. Perhaps the way we have been distinguishing body and mind is misguided.

Star Trek reflects this issue at several levels. There is always a medical practitioner aboard Starfleet vessels, from the cranky Bones McCoy to the holographic doctor on *Voyager*, whose role is healer of the physical body. These characters have a formidable technology at their disposal, but sometimes even this technology fails and characters die. Yet there is never a chaplain aboard a Starfleet vessel; neither is there a visible chapel as such, although one is mentioned in the Original Series. The spiritual needs of a Starfleet crew—if they even exist—are not addressed in any recognizable way.

By default, the function of the spiritual healer falls, in *Next Generation*, to the good counselor, the empath Deanna Troi. To use Q's words in "All Good Things . . ." she produces pedantic psychobabble, that is, she is the company shrink. From Reginald Barclay, a comic figure, to Captain Picard himself, Troi is the one who ministers to the psychologically sick at heart. So powerful has the influence of psychology become in our culture that we are not at all surprised by her presence, although we may be mystified by her function. She is close friends with Doctor Beverly Crusher, but there is no indication that their fields of expertise overlap. The body and the mind are distinct, separate territories.

To its credit, however, Star Trek has been willing to offer alternate scenarios, and to question the assumptions that underlie our culture's body-mind split, by offering examples of religious specialists whose practices unite the body and mind successfully. Often they appear in the exploration of other species' cultures, although the types are familiar to us from the history of religions on Earth. One case is that of the Vulcan priestess T'Pau in "Amok Time" (Original Series, aired September 1967). The Vulcan race, noted for its superior intelligence, cultivates this characteristic by practicing logic. Vulcan culture privileges logic as the favored scientific answer to suffering. Logic by definition precludes alogic, that is, irrationality and emotion. In this view, religion has no basis in fact or logic. It is irrational and emotional (and, for the most part, proud of it). It is remarkable, therefore, that Vulcans not only continue to have religion but also use it as the preferred container for their repressed emotional core. Vulcan history shows that their strong emotional nature would have destroyed them had they not found a way to control it.

The worst fate a Vulcan can imagine is to be overcome by emotion, yet this is precisely what happens to Spock and, apparently, all male Vulcans on a seven-year cycle. It is noteworthy that this buildup of tension and its ritual release occurs in relation to mating, as it often does in human cultures, and that it is religion that traditionally provides the structure and context for these formal mating patterns. Spock is diagnosed by Doctor McCoy as being in mortal danger: If his need is not addressed, then he will die. His physical existence is endangered by a psychological and spiritual crisis.

T'Pau is the character who both represents the Vulcans' strong spiritual core and presides over the resolution of Spock's affliction of body and mind in the ritual of Pon Farr. Her appearance is formidable and her reputation in the Federation is considerable, although the nature of her authority is shrouded in mystery. Carried into the ritual space by bearers, she speaks in the formal, formulaic words of a religious specialist and draws on powers beyond her own and beyond definition. No higher being is identified or invoked. The language of the episode does not refer to this incident as religious practice, although the presentation of the Pan Farr ritual certainly gives the impression of a religious rite. It is reminiscent of forms of religion practiced in Asia (such as Shinto and Confucianism). In some Asian forms of practice, the invocation of deities in the Western sense is not necessarily part of such ritual, and religious specialists need not have a "vocation" in the Western sense of that term. T'Pau is extremely protective of the integrity of the ceremony and will brook no interference in Vulcan beliefs and rituals by Kirk, but she does allow him to risk his life and Spock's to complete the ritual cycle. She then uses her "off-worlder" influence to save the crew from repercussions for their decision to ignore orders and take Spock to Vulcan.

We normally consider those who uphold, study, and embody the formal structures and beliefs of a given religious tradition as belonging to a "priestly class." They are specialists to whom we turn for interpretation of the tradition itself and its applications to human life. The preservation of the formal rites, formal texts, and traditional meanings fall under their jurisdiction, and they are often conservative authority figures. T'Pau fulfills this function admirably. This kind of religious specialist often possesses superior understanding and privileged knowledge. She is able to guide Spock to a resolution of his Pon Farr by understanding him well: It could even be argued that she understands Kirk just as well in this episode and allows McCoy to administer the drug that mimics death so that he and Spock may live. As far as we can tell, the other Vulcans believe Kirk has died and are not particularly concerned. The border between life and death is familiar space to the religious specialist of priestly calling. In such a setting, ritual death and physical death may carry the same significance. Kirk dies, yet he lives. Spock believes he has killed, but his victim revives. Ritual death is enough to achieve the ritual goal; Spock returns to his rational self, Kirk returns to duty, and both Vulcan and Starfleet's requirements are satisfied. Everyone returns to the status quo. The specialist may satisfy all the worlds by her actions, but only if she understands them equally well. T'Pau affirms and upholds Vulcan traditions—in fact she embodies them—thus deserving recognition as a priestess.

A shaman, however, is often a radical individualist. The term comes to us from the Tungus people of Siberia (where some still practice), but it has come to indicate a generic name for a particular kind of religious specialist. Shamans are soul-specialists. They specialize in the life, suffering, and afterlife of that which is considered immortal in the human species. The Greek word *psychopomp*, or "guide of souls," comes closest to the sense of the term. Most indigenous and ancient cultures acknowledged the existence of the soul; some attributed actual physical form to it. In such cultures, illness was understood to be a direct result of a disturbance of the soul caused either by human or spiritual agents. The shaman was the one who had the special power of communing both with the soul of the patient and with the spirits of that other realm. As a result of special training and experience, a shaman might rescue a soul that had been displaced from a person and was "spirited away." The other, related area of expertise for shamans is navigating the realm of the dead. Once a person was deceased, the soul needed to find its way to that other realm, and the journey might be difficult, causing the soul to linger within the world of the living, a potentially dangerous situation for everyone. The shaman was capable of "soul journey," that is, he or she could travel out of the body and serve as a guide for the souls of the dead.

The shamanic function of a Vulcan religious specialist is crystal-clear in the feature film *Star Trek III: The Search for Spock*. Following the death of Spock in *Star Trek II: The Wrath of Khan*, the third film in the Star Trek Series makes a remarkable proposal: Given the right combination of circumstances, it would be possible to bring one of our favorite characters back from the dead, not with the use of extraordinary technology but through special religious techniques. In this story, Kirk comes to believe in the existence of a Vulcan "eternal soul," the *katra*. Despite the sarcasm of the Starfleet commander, and the usual considerable odds against success, Kirk risks everything to return Spock's soul from the body of McCoy, in which Spock placed it before his death, to Spock's body, which is miraculously restored on the Genesis planet. This is death and resurrection in its most fundamental form. All the effort and the risk, however, would be useless if not for the ritual performance of the Vulcan high priestess T'Lar. Given the body of Spock and the body of McCoy, T'Lar acts as a conduit, channeling Spock's *katra* through her own body and back into the "void" of Spock's mind. The mind-melding ability of the Vulcan race is here developed to its highest potential. Placing her hand on the foreheads of both characters and closing her eyes in deep meditation, she works this miracle of the *fal tor pan*, the "refusion," something the Vulcans themselves have heard about only in the myths of their tradition. Successful, she retreats into the distance, leaving us to wonder how something so mysterious and compelling could exist on, of all places, the planet Vulcan.

Star Trek provides us with many examples of similar religious specialists. Our next example comes from the episode "The Empath" (Original Series, aired December 1968). Kirk, Spock, and McCoy have been mysteriously transported to an underground laboratory where they are about to be tortured to death by a superior race, apparently for no purpose whatsoever. As it turns out, the purpose has to do with a beautiful and mysterious female, whom McCoy calls Gem. The traditional shaman is often depicted as a *wounded healer* who must first experience suffering in order to address the suffering of others. Typically, the initiation of a shaman entails a ritual death and resurrection in order to transform the candidate into someone who is willing and able to fulfill the function professionally. The shaman is understood as chosen to take up this vocation, often by being born with specialized skills and traits.

The Gem character fulfills these expectations in several ways. Her race is mute, and it is likely that some telepathy is used among them. She is the unhappy victim—but also the ultimate result—of an experiment run by the superior Vyans; that is, she has been "chosen." If the experiment is successful, she will be capable of guiding her people into a luminous future, saved by those same Vyans from the death of their star system. Thus, she must suffer, but she will be transformed and become an inspiration to many. But first she must prove her ability to grow, to become truly empathic. This is the purpose our Starfleet heroes are to fulfill: Somehow, they must inspire in Gem the desire to grow beyond her native ability, despite the threat of her own suffering and death. Empathy is a quality that surpasses sympathy, or telepathy, for it suggests the potential of one living being to take into herself the reality and pain of another. Out of that intense communion comes the ability to heal.

Gem heals by the "laying on of hands," a method used in religious traditions the world over. As the good doctor observes, "Her nervous system is so sensitive and highly responsive" that "she can actually feel our emotional feelings and responses . . . they become part of her." Such a healer must be willing to take on the pain of another, despite her own fear and instinct for self-preservation. Gem's nervous system actually connects to both Kirk and McCoy to counteract the worst of their symptoms by taking them on herself, then treating them in herself. Such a person is inevitably perceived to be extraordinary, like the "pearl of great price" mentioned at the end of the episode, able to transcend normal human limitations and offer the possibility of transformation or salvation. Such awe-inspiring qualities are usually associated with spiritual expertise. Buddhist Sutras, the sacred texts of the tradition, are often named for jewels, like the Diamond Sutra, for much the same reason.

Of course, this episode is replete with references to Christian imagery and principles. The pearl of great price echoes Matthew 13:46. We observe first Kirk and then McCoy "crucified" by the Vyans as they willingly sacrifice themselves for the salvation of their friends, and for the greater good of Gem's race, although they are unaware of the latter application until later. The Christ figure is also a religious type: Suspension of one's own desires and identity, rejection of ego by religious specialists for the sake of the transformation or enlightenment of others, is a common heroic theme in religions such as Judaism (Moses) and Buddhism (Siddhartha Gautama) as well. The imagery here is designed to resonate strongly in Western Christendom.

Empathy is a quality Star Trek explores in more depth among the Betazoid race. Troi is only one-half Betazoid, as her father was human. She is spared, therefore, some of the dangers that may accompany total empathy, dangers a shaman would know well. In the episode "Tin Man" (*Next Generation*, aired April 1990) we are offered the example of one character whose total empathy has caused him enormous suffering. Tam Elbrun is "a telepath of extraordinary talent, even for a Betazoid." In most Betazoids, Troi teaches us, telepathic gifts develop in adolescence, but sometimes a child is born with telepathic functions "switched on" at birth. Most of these "never live a normal life . . . the noise of other people's thoughts and feelings would be overwhelming to a child." So far, Elbrun fits the description of a mythological type—the divine child—present in many mythologies. But he challenges the type in many ways as well, for he is neither innocent nor charming. He has made mistakes that have resulted in the death of others, and he has no patience with the doubts, suspicions, and accusations that surround him. Shamans may be marginalized by

their communities as a result of difficult (antisocial) characteristics and the dangers associated with their enhanced powers.
Elbrun belongs to this category. He has the healing qualities of
a shaman, as well as the ambivalent personality often associated with such practitioners. But in this story, he seeks his
own deliverance. By enabling the alien to find meaningful existence once again, he achieves his own "salvation." Which is
his top priority? One might call him selfish, self-centered—
which is precisely Picard's diagnosis.

The alien vessel in this episode is named Gomtuu, but
Starfleet calls it "Tin Man." The implications of this name are
important to understand. The Tin Man is a character from our
own mythology that suggests a hollow metal shell with no
heart. As it turns out, of course, in the classic tale *The Wizard
of Oz* the Tin Man had a heart all along but needed a symbol of
that heart in order to be whole or healed. In this episode, a
"mysterious entity"—a ship with no passengers—presents itself to Elbrun as an "intelligence that swims naked through
space like a fish through the sea, totally alien . . . ancient and
alone . . . so lonely for so long." Ancient, alive, mysterious,
powerful, and reaching out for contact, Gomtuu might accu-
rately be described as *numinous*, from a Latin word used to
designate that which is mysterious and more powerful than
human. As is usually true in the history of religions, the different parties involved in this episode view the *numinous* as desir-
able for different purposes: The Romulans want to use it as a
weapon; Starfleet wants to use it to increase its own knowledge and power. Both parties want to use it for their own
ends. Tam Elbrun is the only one who is willing to be used *by*
Gomtuu, because for him this will mean salvation, liberation
from the torturous life he has led, as well as transformation to
a higher plane of existence. As mysterious as Elbrun is to his

colleagues, Gomtuu is to him, and in his experience this is unique. Elbrun is tortured by his inability to bear his unceasing knowledge of all who surround him; he longs for peace. Tin Man wants to die; having no one to care for, it has no reason to exist. When Data questions whether this truly is the purpose of existence, Tam agrees that it is. The symbiotic relationship Gomtuu establishes with its passenger is mutually beneficial and transforming. Data observes that through joining both have been healed; "grief has been transmuted to joy, loneliness to belonging." In short, the shamanic goal of spiritual and physical healing has been accomplished for both through the special powers accessible to religious specialists. When it is all over, they disappear into the oblivion of space, both reborn, but it is beyond our ability to observe the final product.

Tam Elbrun is a rare specimen by most standards. Like Gem, he is a wounded healer, uniquely capable of easing the suffering of others as a result of his own pain. Tam's use of his telepathic and empathetic qualities are shamanic insofar as he uses them to heal suffering and build bridges between worlds (both astrophysical and psychological). But he is a renegade shaman, like those of some Eurasian traditions, who leaves the known world behind. Picard is correct: He is potentially a danger to them all.

The idea that biological and psychological evolution is both natural and continuous in biological life-forms has profound implications for our understanding of ourselves, as well as the ways in which we accept or reject traditional Western religious belief systems. The central character in the *Next Generation* episode "Transfigurations" (aired June 1990), whose true name we never learn, experiences his own evolution. He is called John Doe—an extremely generic title for someone who

is quite extraordinary! "Who, or what, is he?" people keep asking. We meet him in a physical state close to death, but it becomes almost immediately apparent that he is in fact generat-
ing new life. The juxtaposition of life and death is a dominant
theme of this episode, as is usually the case in episodes that
highlight religious specialists.

John Doe is an amnesiac; he does not know his own name
or what is happening to him. His body is in the process of becoming something *totally other*, as the good doctor repeatedly
notices: He is a mystery to himself and everyone else. This
episode uses vocabulary that comes from both biology and religion: the transformation of cell structure, mutation, transmutation, metamorphosis. His effect on others is also transformative. First, Geordi La Forge becomes a better, more effective,
more confident person. Then Doctor Crusher feels "a spiritual
connection" to him, drawn by his "strength and serenity," that
goes beyond the usual intimacy of the doctor-patient relationship—a good potential sex partner or something more? He is
yet another example of the wounded healer, and because
Crusher herself is another version of this theme, having lost
her husband under tragic circumstances and dedicated her life
to helping others, it is possible that John Doe's spectacular
skills in this area add attraction for her. Of course, he also per-
sonifies the quality of charisma, a necessary but not always
trustworthy feature of the religious specialist. Charismatic
teachers and healers populate many traditions and share a certain magnetic personality that is often irresistible. It is this
quality that carries the most danger, as we have repeatedly
seen over time. Once one has been affected experientially by
such a figure, it is hard to be objective about him.

In some ways John Doe, like Gomtuu, represents an unknown, alien life-form with transformative powers; in other

ways, like Elbrun, he could be dangerous, as his own people repeatedly insist. He challenges Doctor Crusher's technological facility and understanding by recovering from his mortal injuries beyond her ability to heal him. Then he crosses the border between being an interesting specimen and becoming a character who can and does act in ways that defy explanation.

In fact, John Doe challenges boundaries of many kinds. Like Gem, he becomes capable of remarkable healing by the laying on of hands, and ultimately he possesses the power to "reverse death" itself. When Worf dies in the attempt to stop him from leaving the ship in a stolen shuttle craft, John Doe restores the body to life with his touch. He increasingly experiences energy surges during which he is flooded with "clarity and purpose," and he visibly glows, but he is in great pain. The agony he experiences is the symptom of his rapidly evolving new powers that enable him to heal. His transformation to a new life-form is projected from the inside (cell structure) out (visible appearance).

The response of his own xenophobic people, the Zalconians, mirrors the common human response to those who are different, who challenge categories, who speak or act with divine or prophetic authority. They accuse him of encouraging dissent, disturbing the "natural order of our society." They are terrified of what they "cannot understand" and invoke the characterization of "evil." They try to kill him and those like him. But he inspires in the *Enterprise* crew both gratitude and wonder, as he finally becomes a being of light. He does not take the *Enterprise* crew on a soul-journey, but he opens the door to a level of understanding not accessible previously. In doing so he embodies the function of prophecy in most religious traditions.

Characteristically, prophets are misunderstood and often made to suffer and die for their vision, which many regard as misguided, deluded, and impossible. Acting on an impulse from a source that cannot be identified, a prophet is one chosen for an extraordinary experience that involves serving as a conduit between the human and the divine or, in this case, the humanoid and the design (or designer) of evolution itself. Although he is a Zalconian and not human, the crew of the *Enterprise*—and as a result we the audience—accept him as close enough to human to serve as a model.

This episode carries considerable significance if we accept the premise, basic to Star Trek, that our current status, rather than being the end or goal of the evolutionary process, is but a step along the way and that a transfiguration such as this might be in our future. Of course, the term "transfiguration" is loaded, for it has been used in many religious traditions in the context of religious transformation. Evolution, then, may be understood not as a challenge to religious tradition but as its fulfillment. This remarkable proposition mirrors our culture's efforts to accommodate both the religious and scientific world views. It may be a cunning compromise, as unscientific as it is irreligious, but as it appears in the body of John Doe, it *works*.

Beyond Healing: Who *Else* Is Out There?

Star Trek offers many visionaries from other species whose abilities echo but transcend those we know from our own history. Guinan, the popular *Next Generation* bartender played by Whoopi Goldberg, appears in a number of episodes and in the film *Star Trek Generations* as the perfect choice to minister to the alcoholic and emotional requirements of those crew members and passengers who cannot or will not appear on Deanna Troi's patient list. As an El-Aurian she is a "listener," but her abilities are more complex. What Guinan hears is often more than is spoken, and what she knows is as a result of listening for more than five hundred years of life. A survivor of the Borg invasion and assimilation of her world, she has traveled the galaxy and even visited nineteenth-century Earth (in "Time's Arrow").

In the episode "Yesterday's Enterprise" (aired February 1990), when the *Enterprise C* is catapulted into the future during a battle with the Romulans, changing history and transforming Picard and his crew in the process, it is Guinan who knows that something is terribly wrong. It is on her advice that Picard sends the crew of the earlier incarnation back to its own time and certain death for most of them. It is her sole-surviving memory that suggests to Tasha Yar that she is not even supposed to be alive (thus sowing the seeds for a series of events that will cause Picard considerable trouble in the future). All of this is terribly convoluted, of course, as tampering with the time line inevitably proves to be. At the center of it all, however, is Guinan, mysterious yet familiar, unyielding yet apparently undemanding, down-to-earth enough to recommend prune juice to Worf, omniscient enough to see the strands of time unraveling and to act in time to preserve them.

Guinan's role in *Generations* is clearly a prophetic one; it might be described as shamanic as well. The premise of the film is centered on one of those "spatial anomalies" famous in Star Trek, called the Ribbon. This phenomenon is actually a threshold, an entrance to another reality called the Nexus. Traveling through space, this anomaly encompasses two freighters shuttling survivors of the El-Auran diaspora to safety. Guinan and another of her species, Soran, experience a transformation in time and space, transported to an existence "inside joy."[3]

Soren, having lost his family to the Borg, is reunited with them in the Nexus. We do not know what Guinan's paradise was, only that when she was "rescued" by the *Enterprise B* it felt as if she were "ripped" from it, unwilling and forever bereft. When Picard confers with her about Soren's purpose and her experience in the Nexus, she prophetically warns him of its overpowering effect; she tells him that once there he will not care about his former life and its responsibilities. We also know that she leaves an "echo" of herself there, for when Picard enters the Nexus later in the film he finds her there to guide him. She is his soul-guide in this other reality. He ultimately rejects that paradise because it is "not real," or perhaps not the reality he prefers, for Star Trek privileges heroes who choose to act in the world we most commonly acknowledge as shared and historically true. Guinan's alter ego, however, continues to exist in the limbo of the Nexus, even as her more tangible presence exists in the limbo of the bar in Ten Forward (but not in the credits of this film). It is a status that seems to suit her.

In the *Next Generation* episode "Where No One Has Gone Before" (October 1987) we are introduced to the character called the Traveler. He clearly has extraordinary powers but, like John Doe, is at the same time vulnerable: He suffers. He has the ability to act as a lens that focuses thought. What he does is perceived as a form of magic by the crew: The difference between magic and religion is often a matter of perception, both on Star Trek and in the experience of Terran religions. Historically, whenever one religious tradition seeks completely to usurp or replace another, it begins by denigrating that religion's common form of belief and practice as based on false assumptions and engaging in "magic." "Magic is what those *other* people do; *we* practice the true faith," has been the claim of many in the history of religions on Earth. This episode raises the possibility that we would perceive as magic the ability of a specialist from another species with powers beyond our comprehension. The point is well taken.

Certainly, the Traveler is familiar in some ways from our previous encounters with religious specialists, but he takes their capabilities to another level. He has tremendous powers that are incomprehensible to us; he has the ability to take the *Enterprise* and its crew not only to another physical reality but also to a place where physical and psychological reality are identical. As a *psychopomp*, he is a guide of souls; he can also alter the very laws of physics. He also allows mistakes to be made that place the *Enterprise* and its crew at serious risk, knowing full well that "the world is not ready for such dangerous nonsense," as the Traveler warns Ensign Wesley Crusher.

If "space and time and thought aren't the separate things they appear to be" (Wesley); if there is a place where "the world of the physical universe and the world of ideas is somehow intermixed" (Picard); and if "thought is the basis of all reality" (the Traveler)—a true *psychopomp* would know how to access and manipulate it. If in such a place and under such conditions "we may lose the ability to distinguish between thought and reality" (Picard), a true *psychopomp* would be the only reliable guide there. When Picard meets his deceased mother, she appears to him to have the answers he seeks, echoing the beliefs of many cultures that the dead possess powers and knowledge that are inaccessible to the living. She wonders, somewhat rhetorically, whether they are "at the end of the universe . . . or the beginning of it." In this place, the boundaries between the realms of thought and those of physical reality—those of space and time—are not the only boundaries that disappear, for so do those between the worlds of the living and of the dead. This is shamanic territory, and, as the Traveler observes, we are not ready to go there.

It is also important to remember that an experience that would be characterized as madness in some contexts might be described as revelation in others. Sometimes it is hard to tell which is true—or whether both might be true simultaneously. Shamans have often been described as being mad. Their experience and training require the ability to transcend ordinary limitations and challenge the conviction that there is only one true reality. The Traveler is apparently aware that his abilities and knowledge sound crazy to most humans: Only Picard and Wesley Crusher really have any clue that he is speaking of another level of being and understanding. When this character reappears in two later episodes, he raises these issues yet again. In "Remember Me" (October 1990) Doctor Crusher is trapped in a "warp bubble" created as an experiment by her son, Wesley. The reality she experiences is constructed unconsciously by her, based on the thoughts she was having at the time of the accident. Only when she realizes the true nature of that reality is she able to be saved from extinction. It is the Traveler who helps guide Wesley to reach his mother and provide her with a path out of oblivion. It might easily be said that the good doctor spends much of this episode in a state of madness. Star Trek provides an alternative (or additional) scenario: While Beverly Crusher is living in a reality of her own creation, those back in the real world of the *Enterprise* have physical proof of its existence—the warp bubble is visible on their computer screen. Of course, that doesn't prove that she is not suffering from temporary insanity. The fact that neither world is really real is icing on the cake. The Traveler has taken us all on a soul-journey, during which some very profound questions about the nature of reality can be raised. In many religions, such a journey is experienced as revelation. It very often drives the subject mad.

Finally, in the episode "Journey's End" (March 1994) it is the Traveler who, in the form of a descendent of North American Indians, ushers Wesley into his own initiation. He meets his dead father, finds the ability to let go of other people's expectations of him, and finds his own powers outside of space and time. He decides to abandon all his previous life-plans and set out on a journey into the unknown, which the Traveler suggests is as much an internal as an external odyssey: It is where the boundaries between what is internal and what is external disappear. Several figures in the history of Terran religions have gone there before. We call them prophets, mystics, and shamans. They, too, are often thought to be mad.

The Dark Side of Religious Power

The category of religious specialists often includes those who are peacemakers, as well as warmakers. The *Next Generation* episode "Man of the People" (October 1992) presents a Lumerian ambassador, Alkar, known for his specific skill in resolving conflict. He is similar in some ways to Tam Elbrun, because both utilize special mental capacity. The Lumerian provides us with the darker, shadow side of empathy, telepathy, and other special psychic powers. We generally *are* suspicious of people with such powers for fear of this potential.

Alkar is immediately drawn to Troi, and Maylor, his "mother," also knows that there is some connection between them that threatens her role. Their special psychic abilities set them apart from others and draw them toward one another; everyone else is out of the loop and will need research and evidence to identify the nature of the dynamic among them. As among shamans and other specialists such as prophets and mystics, they have characteristics that can only be truly recognized by each other; ordinary people may only feel awe tempered by fear.

Deanna Troi immediately senses "something very unusual" in Alkar, a "calmness, serenity, tranquility . . . you seem to embody the very qualities that you hope to draw out in others." At the same time, she senses in Maylor malevolent feelings that are out of proportion with the circumstances. Star Trek often observes that the qualities of humanoid life include a restless, tormented spirit in need of the characteristics Alkar embodies but drawn to those of Maylor, and that in the tension among these qualities lie creativity and the ability to achieve high goals. As a study in extremes, Alkar and Maylor give us a bipolar impression of our identity, focused on the power of emotion. Religion often teaches us to seek peace, to try to balance the extremes that compose our essence. Sometimes, religions succeed where other approaches fail, but in the modern world we have tried a variety of other approaches to this problem. Psychology is the obvious choice for many. The idea of the balance between opposites is discussed in many Asian traditions such as Taoism, Shinto, and the teachings of the South Asian movements such as Sanatana Dharma (Hinduism) and Buddhism.

Alkar employs a "funeral meditation" upon the death of Maylor that provides a lesson in the efficacy of ritual practice. The words are innocuous enough: "An end to grief, an end to pain, strength comes from love, and courage from wisdom." He calls it "one of our most sacred ceremonies," but its effects are not symbolic; they are quite concrete. The nature of the transformation achieved by this ritual has little to do with comfort of the bereaved; rather it achieves a psychic link with Troi as his next victim. His abilities as a peacemaker apparently derive from his ability to establish such a link and then download all of his own emotional negativity through this link into the female receptacle he has chosen.

It is Doctor Crusher who represents the perspective of scientific research in this scenario. Her focus ultimately is on neurotransmitters. She is able to establish a scientific reason for a spiritual/psychological process. Science may be able to help us define the processes by which religious experience occurs, but it may fail to explain the experience itself. This falls into the realm of psychology and ultimately religion: The former would call Troi's experience a form of mental contagion, perhaps, but religion recognizes it as possession. Science ultimately provides the resolution to Troi's problem, of course, and so is absolutely necessary both to the story line and the explanation of these events. Only by reversing the flow of transmissions from Alkar to Troi may she be saved; it will also result in his death. This may only be achieved by convincing him that she is dead, and in order to do so she must die. This episode is replete with dark and troubling images, and Alkar's special abilities inevitably point to madness and death.

The effects of Alkar's special skill upon Troi are physical as well as psychological. They include rapid aging and compulsive behaviors, including out-of-control sexuality. These symptoms belong in the realm of possession, also defined in some contemporary diagnoses as the symptoms of bipolar disorder, sometimes as schizophrenia. Religions often speak of the "casting out of demons" as a cure for madness, and religious specialists often engage in this behavior. Rituals designed to address these situations often require a ritual death and rebirth of the patient. In this episode, it is Doctor Crusher who presides over this process, one of the few examples when she crosses our cultural line between the physical and spiritual realms of healing.

Alkar declares that he needs Troi to "make it possible for me to do my work." He tells Picard that he "needs to be focused, centered, free of dispiriting thoughts" and that he "discovered long ago I had the ability to channel my dark thoughts, my unwanted emotions to others, leaving me unencumbered." He calls these women his "receptacles," and, as Crusher observes, he floods them with his "psychic waste." It is, of course, interesting that he chooses women to fulfill this role. There is precedent in Indo-European cultures, like ancient Greece, Rome, and India, for the image of the female as a vessel; to this day one of the most common representations of a goddess in South Asia is as a clay pot. In that context, this is not necessarily a denigrating or dismissive image; it is one of enormous power, and its sexual aspect is part of its compelling nature. The fact that sexuality, desire, and jealousy are parts of the symptoms shared by his victims confirms Star Trek's judgment in this episode: Such qualities are undesirable in a spiritual relationship of a positive kind. Death and rampant (female) sexuality are simply incompatible with acceptable religious practice in the perspective of this episode. Deanna Troi's descent into a dark caricature of herself—a vamp in dress and attitude—is meant to signal a purely negative result. Far from being empowered by her connection to Alkar, she is destroyed by it. Star Trek is unable or unwilling to imagine an alternate scenario. Some of Troi's symptoms may recall ancient as well as contemporary religious practice elsewhere, just as possession has been known to produce positive results in a variety of religious traditions. But when Alkar is tricked into abandoning Troi, what we see is the casting out of demons, as familiar from the biblical text as it is from *The Exorcist*.

Alkar feels justified in using women in this way because a "higher purpose" is being served, and he states that one must see the "broader canvas" in order to be able to understand. Picard views this as an immoral act, a brutalization. We might ask if it is not true that the sacrifice of a few would be acceptable to achieve peace for, and the survival of, the many. Star Trek debates this issue regularly. How acceptable is personal sacrifice under such circumstances, and what does the history of religions tell us about this? Perhaps if Troi had been given a choice, then it might have made all the difference. The darker side of religious specialists and their powers has always been located in the realm of choice and application. Whether such figures and their assistants go willingly and with full preparation into this radical and demanding form of practice, and how they apply what insight they gain thereby, determines whether their behavior is acceptable, either in Star Trek or in life.

"Oh My God, It's Full of Stars"

Finally we must explore imagination, science, and the potential promise of the religious specialist. Humankind has used the heavens as a screen upon which to project our deepest fears as well as our deepest hopes since the beginning of human history on Earth. The fact that a screen may now be located in the living room does not alter the power of the projection. Astrology is one example of this psychological process: It is the human mind that constructs "constellations," connects the dots. We attribute further meaning to what we see by according significance to our relationship to those constellations: when we were born, how those stellar objects move over the course of time in relation to us, what we might learn by extrapolating from those observations. There are many, still, who organize their lives by the stars and have complete confidence in their meaning, if only that meaning could be interpreted properly. This vast construction of meaning has worked over thousands of years and cannot be dismissed lightly.

Whether religiously or scientifically determined, our worldviews inevitably include the sky—"the heavens," as we call it.[4] In our desperate moments scientists and believers alike gaze skyward, in the hope of aid, solace, or understanding. In paranoid moments, some believers as well as purveyors of popular culture imagine monsters (animate, inanimate, whatever) coming from the same place, as in much recent popular cinema. In optimistic moments, these same people may imagine powerful beings with extraordinary powers who will help find whatever is lacking, and this was one of Roddenberry's favorite themes, as it has been for Steven Spielberg and George Lucas. It is common to attribute superior status to that which is able to manipulate what humans cannot: space, time, the flow of events. If such figures are not acknowledged as divine, they may usefully be characterized as religious specialists. And whether these beings participate in the creative or the destructive aspect of extraordinary power is a judgment that should not be made too quickly. As the Tao, the religions of India, and Star Trek occasionally suggest, the universe may prefer balance. What may appear to be dark may lead ultimately to light. The monsters, the divine powers, the alien beings: in short, whatever may exist out there likely has its own agenda; trying to imagine what that agenda might be is always the problem.

Over the years Star Trek has presented an assortment of religious specialists who, like Anij in *Insurrection*, are Western types but may be creatively and productively viewed through an Eastern lens. Star Trek's popularity in Asia is partly a result of the producers' decisions to include characters of Asian descent, but it is also a product of the franchise's tendency over thirty-plus years to incorporate images and ideas that are familiar to non-Western audiences. The worldview of Starfleet and the Federation may be overwhelmingly Western, but there are other voices here as well, and some of them offer considerable insight Star Trek provides an opportunity to explore possibilities unknown to normative Western perspectives, rather than be limited by what is familiar. If those possibilities lead to paradox (as in "All Good Things . . . "), it is useful to remember that the Zen koan (as in the classic question "What is the sound of one hand clapping?") prizes paradox as a means to deeper understanding. The fact that the architecture of the Ba'ku is familiar to us from Buddhism—with its stupas that imitate the topknot of the Buddha himself—and that their lifestyle and special skills are familiar from Tibet, might be interpreted as a form of Orientalism, using what is convenient from the East for our own purposes with no regard for its intrinsic integrity. The Ba'ku are an unmistakably white, Anglo people, and Anij is a very Western woman. Q is unmistakably white, obnoxiously Western, and close enough to the false prophet on occasion to arouse and deserve all the disdain heaped upon him by the *Enterprise* crew. However, he also affords us an opportunity to discover the role of the Trickster of Native American cultures. The presence in popular culture of influences from non-European cultural and religious heritage cannot be denied. How we might explore and accommodate such influences without denigrating their sources—how we might acknowledge and value their presence while accepting them on their own terms—is the challenge of the twenty-first century and beyond. Star Trek has observed the culture wars of the twentieth century and proposed some alternatives. It is one of the few places in our culture that the effort may be made in the popular media. For these reasons, Star Trek is worthy of close attention.

If the characters introduced in this chapter can be characterized as religious specialists, we might hypothesize yet another function for them in the Star Trek context that may prove intriguing. After all, Star Trek itself claims to take us "where no man, or no one, has gone before." The phrase in the Original Series was "where no man has gone before"; by the debut of the *Next Generation* series, the need for gender- and species-sensitive language necessitated the substitution of "no one." Star Trek accommodated inclusive language better suited to its own context; the gist of the phrase, however, remained constant. It is that sense of providing a companion, or a guide into the unknown, that is the defining quality of the religious specialist. Shamans take the ill, the lost, the dead, and the living on a journey that is both internal and external—a "soul-journey." Its purpose is to heal, to recover, to make whole, to make over, to transform. The geography is always circular, for as *Voyager's* crew knows, the goal is ultimately to return home. However the effect of the journey is so radically transformative that nothing, or no one, will ever be the same again, and even "home" must be redefined. In these respects, we might view Star Trek's mission statement as a blueprint for growth in a pluralistic universe. Clearly, it has concluded that there *is* a role for religious specialists in the future it envisions, as there is in the present and has been in the past on Earth. Perhaps an examination of these figures may offer us, as the viewing audience, a singular opportunity to explore beyond the familiar manifestations of religions in the traditions we know to the extraordinary dimensions of religions in traditions known and unknown to us. To engage in the cross-cultural study of such phenomena requires a serious journey, to be sure, but one replete with the "unknown possibilities of existence."

4

Enterprise Engaged: Mythic Enactment and Ritual Performance

SUSAN L. SCHWARTZ

Although most of the *Enterprise* crew does not appear to practice a religion or promote any myth other than the overarching one of Starfleet itself, Gene Roddenberry's vision does not preclude the possibility of other cultures doing so. And unlike our current Western ideology, which suggests that myth, ritual, symbol, and the accoutrements of religiosity are inconsistent with technological advancement and its prerequisite of rational, logical thought, several episodes present scenarios in which such ideas and practices coexist with space travel and technological advancement.

In the episode "Darmok" (September 1991), an entire civilization whose mythology defines and dominates their language reaches out to Captain Jean-Luc Picard, who successfully makes a connection by telling the story of Gilgamesh. These "children of Tamar" are capable of outmaneuvering the *Enterprise* and, perhaps to satisfy a cowboy ethic, of outshooting it as well. The Klingons, of course, possess a rich, heroic mythological base, one that constantly challenges but also supports the characters Worf and B'Elanna Torres in the religiously sterile Starfleet milieu. And from the earliest episodes of the original Star Trek series, we have known that the supremely logical Vulcans rely on a highly developed esoteric complex of myth and ritual observance. It thus can be argued that Star Trek projects into the future the possibility that imagery, practices, and ideas associated with religion are viable after all.

Replicating Rich and Varied Ingredients

A culture's mythos, defined here as sacred story, contains the imagery and metaphor that define it. Across cultures, we see thematic parallels embedded in mythology, and the fascination of such shared motifs has fueled interest and controversy. The popularity of Joseph Campbell's work illustrates how compelling such comparative studies can be, although their legitimacy must always be questioned. The differences among traditions and mythologies are as interesting and important as their similarities.

Myth is more compelling than legend, more definitive than saga or folk tale, because it engages a group, culture, or society on a deeper level. Often myth will refer to characters who live and events that occur in a different time, on another plane of reality; myth often describes divine figures whose actions are definitive in the creation of the world. Despite our very Western, modern conviction that myth implies falsehood, it remains the basis for most societies and their religious traditions. We can insist that what cannot be proven scientifically has no reality, but we continue to tell stories and to believe them on some level. Star Trek is a vast modern mythos, and even though it is not historically true, it contains compelling qualities that keep it alive despite the fickleness of American culture and its search for the rational, factual, and real.

Myths are therefore associated with cultural worldviews, that is, collective understandings of the world constructed over time by diverse members of a culture. Myths are accepted as authoritative descriptions of the sources, goals, and meanings of a society. They may also describe an anticipated future of a society, for better or for worse. Therefore, myths are important indicators of how people within a given culture understand the world and themselves. Their authority can derive from a divine source, or from their age or traditional status, or simply from the fact that they are widely accepted. This authority helps them transcend the fact that they often become understood within the culture as having an essential authority that transcends the individual authority of the mythmakers. Myths are important indicators of how people within a given culture understand the world and themselves. The authority of a culture's myths usually transcends the fact that they often contradict themselves in ways large and small. Some differences are due to local or political factors, and in primarily oral cultures, where so many myths originate, the *variants*, or alternate versions of a single episode, serve to enrich the mix; the story will change to accommodate the needs of the audience.

The issue of truth, then, can be tricky, even within a single religion. Within cultures such as ours—with a variety of religions actively present—interpretations and perceptions become fluid. Perhaps that is why myth has come to suggest a more elastic or deceptive form of truth (as it appears in modern print media, for example). But for most of human history, among the many traditions of the world myth has been the repository of truth: not literal, historical, or scientific truth but a larger, more important kind of truth, one that lies beyond the challenge of empirical evidence. Its strength lies in its ability to discern and describe truths about the nature of humanity, often in relation to divinity. The use of the term "myth" here refers to this cultural sense of the term, without concern for issues of literal or historical veracity.

"Ritual" is another challenging and controversial term. It describes actions and behaviors in religious contexts that may be believed capable of producing concrete or symbolic results. Currently, there is lingering suspicion regarding religious ritual among those who doubt its efficacy, or reject its structured formality, or question its use of objects. Expressions such as "empty and meaningless ritual" have been associated with a host of religious traditions from Hinduism to Catholicism, and it was the suspicion of such practices that contributed to the Protestant Reformation in Europe. To make matters even worse for ritual, Sigmund Freud noted the similarity between the compulsive behaviors of his neurotic patients and the repetitive, structured activities of religious adherents and proceeded to develop his conclusion that religion itself was a neurosis characterized by such behaviors.

This chapter seeks to explore the implications of the ways in which Star Trek represents ritual. The series of TV episodes and films has characterized ritual as certain ceremonial, formal, and formulaic behaviors associated with a shift in mood, a change of situation, or a transformation of an individual or group, usually in association with a crisis of some kind. Star Trek does not necessarily identify rituals as belonging to a particular religion—or any religion at all (it may not even include a reference to a deity or higher authority). Ritual in Star Trek therefore serves to reinforce the operative myth of those who practice it. This is science fiction, after all, and the writers are less concerned with approximating actual religious practice than with providing compelling entertainment. However, the writers do not exist in a vacuum. Accordingly, the ways in which Star Trek represents myth and ritual in action can offer useful insight into American ambivalence toward the religious roots, and contemporary viability, of these phenomena.

Peter Pan Meets the Taoist Master

Star Trek VI: The Undiscovered Country begins with a cataclysm, a horrific explosion of the Klingon moon Praxis, which was the *practical* solution to the demands of a warrior people for unlimited energy. Overmining and a lack of precaution bring the Klingon Empire to the brink of extinction. The Vulcan ambassador Sarek initiates peace talks that propose to end generations of hostilities that the Klingons can "no longer afford." Sarek's son, Spock, pursues this initiative and offers the soon-to-be-retired *Enterprise* and its crew as an escort for the Klingon leader, Chancellor Gorkon, as he and his party approach Earth for a summit. This film contains the tried and true formulas that have worked for Star Trek over time, with the original crew reunited for one last adventure. But it also offers the possibility of a different reading, for this is a film about the passage of time, prejudice, rigidity, and failure of imagination: How might Starfleet conceive of life without its archenemy?

The film bears a clear reference to the events in the former Soviet Union, the nuclear accident at Chernobyl, and the disintegration of the "evil empire," as the Soviet bloc had come to be viewed by some in the West.

This is also a story of betrayal by those who cannot cope with change. Trust is an elusive commodity at such times. Following the catastrophe, events follow quickly, and characters retreat into familiar patterns of behavior that are dubious at best. Military types like Klingon General Chang and the Starfleet admirals resort to violence. Kirk, restrained from action at first by the power of Spock's presence and guidance, and later because he is arrested and jailed, cannot hold his tongue. His fierce mistrust of and hatred for the Klingons is recorded by Lieutenant Volaris, to be used against him at his trial. "It never occurred to me," he admits later, "to trust Gorkon."

It is Spock who provides the balancing factor to all this instinctual behavior. Spock is the thoughtful, philosophical presence who knows what actions may be useful and where logic may be fruitful, but he also knows the limitations these formulas impose. He has some remarkable things to say. Early on, during his meeting with Volaris, a Vulcan whose training at Starfleet Spock sponsored, we are privy to a Vulcan ritual toast. Spock wears monklike robes, she, her uniform. Candles are lit, chalices are raised. When she remarks upon the painting in his quarters, Marc Chagall's *Expulsion from Paradise*, he states that he keeps it because "it serves as a reminder that all things must end." When she takes this as a cue to discuss her own concerns about the future of the balance of power between Starfleet and the Klingons, he has a more cosmic view in mind—and reveals his spiritual side. "You must have faith

. . . that the universe will unfold as it should," he tells her, but this generates some anxiety in Volaris, who appeals to logic as all good Vulcans would. Spock, however, has experienced much in his life; he has died and been reborn, mind-melded with endless alien life-forms, meditated long and hard. "Logic," he informs her, "is the beginning of wisdom, not its end." Knowing actor Leonard Nimoy's tendency to adapt the occasional gesture or phrase from Hebrew scriptures into his characterization of Spock, those familiar with the proverbs might hear in these words a resonance: The fear of the Lord is the beginning of wisdom. But here Spock adds, "You must have faith . . . that the universe will unfold as it should." That is, the universe is in process; it has its own path, oblivious and impervious to our efforts at control or even understanding. One should flow with it rather than against it, which would lead only to defeat. Spock's words are familiar to us from such Eastern traditions as Taoism (China), Divine Dharma (India), and Zen Buddhism (Japan).[1]

There is a Peter Pan reference at this film's end ("First star to the left, and straight on 'til morning"), a comment on Western fantasies of eternal youth and failed maturity, balanced by Spock's older, more reflective approach to the universe. Neither has exclusive claim to effectiveness. But as suggested by the Tao, the goal is defined as balance between different modes of being and understanding. *Undiscovered Country*, after all, is a line from Shakespeare's *Hamlet*, (Act III, scene 1), and its original referent was not to the "future" or to unexplored external geography but to inner geography and to death ("all things must end"). When Star Trek strives to engage us on this level, it offers insight beyond its apparent entertainment value.

Dressing Warmly on
Other Planes of Existence

By the last season of the *Next Generation* TV series, the writers, actors, and producers were often at their best, playful, willing to take on characters and concepts boldly. To the delight of some and the disgust of Wesley Haters, the character of Doctor Beverly Crusher's son reappeared in an episode titled "Journey's End." The episode offers much in the realm of religion studies, presenting rites of passage, religious specialists, and yet another shift of perspective in Star Trek's approach to religion.

Most religions acknowledge the importance of the phases of life, that is, the recognition that each lifetime contains a series of transitions from one status to another. The most common of these include birth, the entrance into adulthood, marriage, parenthood, old age, and death. Religions characteristically provide rites of passage on such occasions.[2] "Journey's End" is one large rite of passage, part of *Next Generation's* end as a TV phenomenon. It is also a rite of passage for Wesley, Picard, and the generically portrayed North American Indians. The entire story is set in a liminal area of space: Demilitarized zones and neutral zones are physical manifestations of what people experience as being in-between, where the dangerous and vulnerable characteristics are tangible.

The events in "Journey's End" include the arrival of a strangely surly Wesley, who ultimately rejects Starfleet Academy and everyone's expectations (including those of his surrogate father, Picard, and his mother) that he would follow in his father's footsteps. At the same time, the *Enterprise* must deal with a group of intractable American Indians who refuse to abandon a planet, Dorvan V, they had found some time before; the Cardassians now have rights to it as a result of a treaty endorsed by Starfleet. The powers that be in Starfleet Command are equally rigid, refusing to reconsider the treaty in light of these realities. In short, almost everyone is unwilling to reconsider the assumptions by which they operate, the rules by which they direct their attitudes and behavior, and the roles they have always played. Picard must find a way out of the impasse among the tribal people, Starfleet, and the Cardassians; Wesley must address his growing need for another kind of life despite the pressure from Picard and Beverly Crusher. It is, indeed, a journey's end for many of these separate parties, but it also signals a beginning for most.

The interaction between Picard and Anthwara, the tribal leader, tells us that Picard's own convictions about the nature of religious belief and practice are a part of what limits his ability to cope with their circumstances. When he states, "I have the deepest respect for your beliefs and the meaning they hold for your people," Picard's attitude differs noticeably from those of the European invaders of the Americas from the fifteenth century onward. However, he is unprepared to accept the possibility that their choice of Dorvan Five was not simply a matter of environmental conditions. Anthwara states, "When I came here twenty years ago, I was welcomed by the mountains, the rivers, the sky." Picard is respectful but unable to make the leap. Starfleet Admiral Nechayev, Picard's superior, makes the same mistake that invaders of indigenous peoples have always made: "They are a nomadic group; they never should have gone there in the first place."

The assumption that nomadic peoples wander aimlessly and can just as well be one place as another discounts their deep relationship with the land and the fact that it is, for them, an interactive relationship. This episode does not, however, dismiss the possibility that there may be truth in Anthwara's words. The question is left open. Anthwara probes for the history of Picard's own family, and it is clear that the strength and history of his family are of great importance to him, perhaps as important as they are for the Indian tradition, but in a different way. Anthwara states, "We have strong ties to our ancestors . . . we believe that their actions guide us even now." He discovers that in 1690, when the Spanish took revenge for the Pueblo Revolt of 1680, a man named Picard was responsible for the deaths and suffering of many ancestors. He believes that this Picard has been sent into this situation "to erase a stain of blood," for "nothing that happens is truly random." Picard replies that he does not see how "something that happened over 700 years ago can have any bearing."

Although troubled by the possibility that a "dark chapter" in his family's history might be repeated, he is unable to make the leap and see the connection as Anthwara does. There is, in American culture, a resistance to the suggestion that some things are inevitable, that we do not have complete control or free will. Picard embodies this attitude. Again, the question is left open to interpretation, for what Anthwara has predicted does, in fact, come to pass. He is more than a leader of his people in the political sense of the term. He has the insight, the knowledge, and the respect accorded to a religious leader, and he slowly draws Picard into an experience that raises questions about some very basic assumptions made by Western cultures. More than this, he provides for Picard an *experience* of the power of his beliefs in the nature of history, the connectedness of events and people, and the meaning of seemingly unrelated facts and ideas. Despite his reservations, Picard is made a participant (albeit an unwilling one) in the worldview of this small tribe. By the end of the episode, he is willing to leave them to their own devices as they request and to convince the powers that be in Starfleet to acquiesce. He does not join them, but he has been changed.

The character of Lakanta in this episode is particularly interesting. He actually turns out to be the Traveler, in his third series appearance. We notice that he serves as a shamanic guide, as in his previous episodes. He has come for Wesley and provides an initiation ritual—the "vision quest"—practiced by some Native American groups. Wesley sees a vision of his deceased father, who releases him from the obligation of becoming a Starfleet officer like his parents (and almost everyone else he knows). When Wesley wonders afterward whether this encounter was choreographed by the Traveler, he is told that what happened to him in the "Habak" came "from your own mind, your own spirit." Does that fact make it more or less *real*? Has he been hallucinating? Does his vision carry the authority of genuine religious experience?

The episode is reluctant to judge or even to explore the difference. What is clear is that the experience is authentic for Wesley, who changes his life as a result of it. This ambivalence reflects North American attitudes today. External or divine authority is hard to come by; personal impact is the decisive factor. The Traveler's counsel to Wesley after he has "pulled" himself out of time, and remains worried about the fate of those embattled on the planet, is this: "They must find their own destiny . . . have faith in their ability to solve their problems on their own." Destiny? Faith? In Star Trek? It seems that some fairly important religious concepts are being suggested here that run counter to our usual expectations. Could it be that the secular humanism that defined the series from its inception grew to include such unscientific ideas as these? There is no deity mentioned, to be sure, and the faith and destiny extolled by the Traveler do not appear to rely upon divine authority.

The use of such vocabulary seems to suggest, however, that a major character in the series chooses to embark on a quest for knowledge and experience that lie beyond normal reality as usually defined by Star Trek.

Wesley is about to become a mystic, a type of religious specialist. Mystics are often identified by their choice to withdraw from the ordinary plane of existence, and that is precisely what Wesley must do. Following the Traveler's recommendation, he will begin his education with the Indians on the planet, for he can "learn a lot from these people. They are aware of many things." Picard has been given a brief exposure to their world, but it is Wesley, for better or for worse, who will come to know it deeply, through his own experience. The fact that the writers have condensed and distorted Native American traditions in this episode should not be ignored. But for once in popular media, the richness and depth present there are accorded some legitimacy. And for Star Trek, this is a rather startling shift of perspective.

Ritual Masks and Transformation in Sacred Space

In the episode "Masks" from the final season of *Star Trek: The Next Generation*, written by Joe Menosky, an artifact from an ancient civilization begins a ritual transformation of the *Enterprise* and two crew members; all are thereby required to sacrifice their twenty-fourth century identities. At first the alien object appears to be a comet, encased in ice and cosmic vapors. But the *Enterprise* melts away the outer shell with a phaser blast, and what emerges is an object that proves quite powerful, enough to hold the ship and its crew in limbo, incapable of moving away or severing the connection forged by the object. The only way out of their transformation is through it: The ship must become a temple, and the characters must become masked embodiments of alien solar and lunar deities in order for a verbal ritual exchange to occur. Computer-generated icons double as religious symbols and catalysts of this transformation, merging technology with spiritual meaning in a cosmological, ritual search for balance. Held captive by this interactive alien archive, Picard and crew are forced to decipher its language and its purpose before the starship becomes completely dysfunctional.

The location of this drama is, of course, the celestial sphere, Star Trek's own sacred space. The android Data and Captain Picard are compelled to perform the starring roles in this ritual cosmology, the structure and content dictated by a formidable "other" located outside themselves, ancient and mysterious in origin, with its own agenda, moving in mysterious ways. Only by engaging with it actively—that is, ritually—can its agenda be understood. The episode suggests that the power of ancient forms lives on in the technological future and that such power can coexist with equally powerful technology. Ignorance of these forms and how to engage them is as deadly in the Star Trek future as it is in our own past and present.

It is significant that this episode opens with the android Data, an artificial life-form devoid of emotion but burdened by a longing to be human. In many episodes his dispassionate persona serves as a foil for human irrationality, a screen upon which much is projected by others. As a supreme technological achievement, he is both our hope and our fear of what we might accomplish or become. Usually sexually functional as male, in this episode he is androgynous, that is, both genders, for he becomes the Goddess of the Sun, as well as her father, as well as a variety of other characters. In addition, Data is a "motherless child," a product of engineering, but in mythological terms his is an *unnatural* or *miraculous* birth, for he is "not born of woman." Although designed to resemble his human creator, Doctor Noonien Sung, he has no memory of his creator's wife, his surrogate mother ("Inheritance"). Such figures abound in ancient mythologies worldwide, and they often signal the recognition of a prodigal child or a "chosen one." The android also struggles to achieve some form of creativity, and has recently developed the ability to dream (*"Phantasms"*), an eventuality anticipated by Doctor Soong. Data is a fascinating character on many levels, and in this episode he fulfills much of his potential. When at the end he wonders if he has been dreaming again, we are returned to the ambiguities of myth, dream, ritual, and symbol. Virtual realities jostle for position. What *really* happens here?

As a sophisticated positronic matrix, a living and sentient computer, Data is uniquely vulnerable to the phenomenon encountered here, which turns out to be an alien archive with an active interface, 87 million years old. As the episode begins, Data is struggling to be "creative." In the ship's art studio, he endeavors to sculpt in clay something original, not an exact copy of objects he knows, but some individual interpretive creation. The signal that something has changed is his spontaneous creation of a mask, in a style and of an essence alien to him and to everyone else. At the same time, objects of a similar aesthetic sensibility begin to appear elsewhere on the ship. Computer screens begin to display a series of icons—in both a technological sense and in the mythological or theological sense—that are clearly alien to the ship's systems. Commander William Riker observes, as many would, that "they all look the same . . . primitive and nonfunctional." But Picard, who in previous episodes has emerged as quite an accomplished archaeologist as well as a devotee of detective stories, counters that they are "ceremonial and deceptively simple." It is his insight into the ritual nature of these symbols that will ultimately resolve the conflict of the episode. He recognizes as familiar the use of the sun and the four directions in the cosmological representations appearing on his ship. When Data is able to read the icons as symbolic of "boundary, border, message, messenger, and death," Picard interprets them correctly as related symbols of passage and transformation. This archive, he observes, "is a library designed to do more than communicate information."

Indeed, more transformations of the ship's components follow. Doctor Crusher discovers that "apparently it [the archive] can transform molecular structure and DNA into anything it wants." The most striking transformation, however, is to Data. He feels increasingly uneasy and wonders if he is "losing his mind." The ship's counselor, the empath Deanna Troi, offers the conclusion that he has developed the "android equivalent of multiple personalities." Transformation in a ritual context is presented as a form of madness, the ultimate challenge to a perfect target, this being of perfect logic. Not only does Data psychologically *become* many people in thought and action; he changes physically as well. His forehead sports a highly stylized third eye. Superimposed on his stark Starfleet uniform is a series of what archaeologists know as pectorals, ornate plates on his chest, which change with his personalities. The guiding force in these metamorphoses is the alien archive, which directs the contents of an appropriately named "transformation program" at the ship. And the goal of the archive is to activate a solar mythology that requires ritual catharsis. The reigning solar deity emerges as the goddess Masaka, and the only promise of resolution lies in the personification of her lunar counterpart, Corgano. Her symbol, or icon, is clearly the sun while his is less identifiable. It appears to be a horn, at first, to those engaged in the struggle to interpret the symbol. But it proves to be the crescent moon, an insight provided by Picard's correct analysis, for he knows that cosmologies (stories about the origins and meanings of the world) often require that a balance between powers be maintained.

All the power, in the scenario played out on the *Enterprise*, seems to reside with Masaka, who has been "awakened" by contact with the ship. Data's multiple personalities describe her as cruel, harsh, uncompromising. She clearly demands human sacrifice, and one of Data's personae must serve, although Picard offers himself, thinking thereby to satisfy her and win release of his ship. Legend has it, as recounted by Data, that she dismembered her own father and used his bones to make the world. The *Enterprise* itself is being dismembered at the molecular level and used to create a world, too. As Picard increasingly perceives the risk to his reality, his response perfectly parallels Western European culture's first defense. A photon torpedo is prepared to destroy the archive. But the missile's guiding mechanism becomes dysfunctional, and when opened for examination, it is full of live snakes. Not only can it not fire—it has become a vessel for another form of attack altogether, this time against the *Enterprise* itself. At last, an "other culture" that can effectively defend itself using live symbols of transformation! Snakes have served as transformative symbols of the interface between life and death, healing and immortality, in a great many cultures, from South Asia to ancient Greece to the Americas. It still appears on the caduceus, the symbolic image of the medical profession.

As control and logic increasingly fail aboard the *Enterprise*, that is, in the microcosm (the smaller, human reality), it becomes clear to Picard that something must occur on the macrocosmic level (the divine, or larger, "big picture" reality), within the myth they are living, to resolve the tension. The world created by the probe appears incompatible with the world of the *Enterprise*: One cosmology, or creation, challenges the other. Like the detective he portrays in other episodes, Picard perceives this mystery as a puzzle to be solved, which has always defined our approach to other cultures. The icons are clues for him, as used in computer programming, to access an alternate reality, a truly virtual reality in this case. There is a fundamental ambivalence in his ability to understand, his attempt to decipher the mystery, resolve the dilemma, disperse the tension—and in his ultimate goal, which is to restore *his* version of reality or, to use the vocabulary of the episode, to "disable the transformation program."

Remarkably, the tension is resolved by ritual performance; the appropriate response occurs with the use of masks and ritual. The crew manages to access the transformation program and manipulate it as the archive itself requires. The required image is described in archaic and formulaic language: "A line, as the unending horizon; a curve, as the rolling hillside; a point, as a distant bird; a ray, as the rising sun." Once the image is accessed through the transformation program, the Temple of Masaka itself is created in part of the ship. Picard becomes Corgano, the lunar deity, Masaka's partner and nemesis, by wearing a mask provided by the program. Data's final transformation is into the Sun Goddess herself, utilizing the mask he himself produced in the first moments of the episode. Standing opposite each other on a raised platform, equal in height, Corgano confronts Masaka and their proper relationship is verbally reinstated in a highly ritualized dialogue. They will once more be pursuer and pursued, hunter and prey, alternating their roles in the cycles of day and night, meeting dramatically in moments of solar and lunar eclipse. Their final exchange, establishing this relationship as the hoped-for ideal, provides the ritual catharsis required by the archive and, by extension, the culture from which it originated those many millions of years ago. The ship, Data, and Picard resume their usual Star Trek masks; they return to "normal." The tractor beam, emanating from the archive and attached to the *Enterprise* like an umbilical cord, is released. The transformation program can now be disabled, so that archaeological teams from Starfleet can examine it safely without losing control. What survives is Data, a living memory of what possessed him, and the mask of the Sun Goddess he produced in that original moment of true inspiration. He observes that now, in some sense, he is lonely.

Where else in American popular culture could we possibly find such a treasure trove? Nothing in this episode is beyond evidence we already possess of religions in cultures past and present. From the style of the artifacts, we might posit Mesoamerican and South American influence, that is, Aztec and Inca. The strong solar mythology, the harshness of the sun, and the requirement of human sacrifice support this contextualization. Female solar deities are not numerous but they do occur, in the Shinto tradition of Japan, for example. And in South Asia, the goddess is famous for her creative and devouring essence. The third eye, apparent on Data's forehead, is very South Asian in nature, appearing in most iconography representing the deities and closely linked to solar mythology and the sacred fire. Masks, of course, are at the root of ritual and drama, both of which are fundamental to this episode. As is often the case with masks, what is hidden is also revealed: We learn much about the nature of the android and the Frenchman Jean-Luc Picard by their use of these solar and lunar facades—much about *our* culture, as well.

Normally, of course, we describe such religious paraphernalia and ritual phenomena as alien, precluding Western-style rationality and progress. Our hunger for scientific proof has rendered us completely suspicious of such things. How wonderful, then, how truly paradoxical, to have the epitome of cold reason and logic (Data) fall victim to possession by the irrational in female form (Masaka), powerful, devastating, scalding. Wonderful, too, to have the use of masks—often viewed by Western monotheistic culture as insidious, even satanic—presented as crucial. Masks suggest polytheism and polytheism suggests masks, for the possibilities are infinite and always in flux; transformation awaits. There are two deities present in this episode, but many more wait off-stage. What at first appears innocuous—like the comet that encapsulates the archive until the *Enterprise* trains its own third eye upon it—may prove the catalyst for yet another icon, another avatar, another ritual to another deity, another cosmos with yet a different cosmology.

Darmok Is to Gelad as Dathan Is to Picard

In the episode "Darmok," the *Enterprise* meets the "children of Tamar," otherwise known as the Tamarians, who were judged "incomprehensible" in earlier encounters with Starfleet. Picard in particular, and the command crew to a lesser extent, are forcibly engaged by Dathon, the Tamarian captain, in a ritualized enactment of Tamarian mythology. Dathon risks everything in this attempt, dying a ritual and a physical death in the process. Why he does so should be clear to us: The quest to connect with others, in this case the Federation, no matter how different (or how obtuse) they may be, is a basic humanoid need. Communication is the most basic purpose of myth and may produce a category of behavior and belief that Dathan and his race know particularly well.

The Tamarians speak in metaphors that the *Enterprise* cannot interpret, and, as Data discovers, "the Tamarian ego-structure does not seem to allow what we normally think of as self-identity." Like the Borg in this respect, Dathan is not thinking of himself as he embarks on this mission; it is the good of his people that occupies him. There are, of course, human cultures that emphasize the group rather than the individual, and this theme appears in Star Trek on many occasions, the most outstanding of which may be the question of whether "the good of the many outweighs the good of the few, or the one," in the second and third Star Trek films, *Wrath of Khan* and *Search for Spock*. Many Asian traditions, including Sanatana Dharma (Hinduism) and Buddhism, actually seek to destroy the ego altogether, and this achievement is understood as the gateway to enlightenment and liberation. Their mythologies are full of examples of those who choose a road away from ego-based fulfillment and toward the achievement of nonselfhood, the extinction of desire, the recognition of identity with a larger truth.

The Tamarians live inside their mythology, which serves as a primary vessel of metaphor. They acknowledge individual identity only to the extent that it represents or reflects the image of their mythological prototypes. Only when there is the story of Picard and Dathon at El-Adril do these two characters become *really real*. They transcend their finite, individual existence in the microcosm and enter into the realm of the macro-cosm. In effect, Dathan comes truly alive only after he is dead. This is a common theme in religious mythology, and its power to move people cannot be overstated. Individual death is dwarfed in comparison to the transformation into myth, and the suggestion that what dies may also live. Myths of self-sacrifice for a greater good—and to reveal a more profound understanding of the forces that shape our world—are among the most compelling in the world.

The ritual elements of Picard and Dathon at El-Adril reveal the mythological context of the Tamarian's actions. What is Dathon really doing when he circles the fire? In South Asian wedding ceremonies, the couple circumambulates the fire seven or more times to establish their new identity as a couple before Agni, the god of the sacred flame. In fact, the action of walking itself may be understood as a creative act, as among the Australian Aborigines. Their walkabout has as its purpose the sustenance of the created world. Dathan places four sacred objects in the four corners of his camp, marking the four cardinal directions. He may well be establishing a zone of safety for himself in this ritual, asking for the protection of the divine realm. He is "making" his space sacred. Most religious structures we know require the careful orientation of the building in reference to the four directions, and in the overwhelming majority of cases the most sacred spot, perhaps an altar, faces east (although the direction of choice in China is south). That part of the sky in which the life-giving sun rises has been holy among humans from the earliest times, and its power is often understood as primary, as it is in "Masks."

At the end of this episode, Picard is in his ready room reading the ancient Greek *Homeric Hymns*, which he calls "one of the root metaphors of our own culture." He adds: "More familiarity with our own mythology might help us to relate to theirs." The epic of Gilgamesh, which he had used on the planet in his final, successful effort to connect with the Tamarian, is another example of an ancient mythology that lives on in a culture—namely, ours—that has largely forgotten its existence. Gilgamesh is the prototype of the Western hero, the king of the ancient city Uruk. Variants, or alternate versions, of his story appear in ancient Sumerian, Akkadian, and other texts; it also contains a flood story that parallels the biblical tale of Noah to an astonishing degree. Like Darmok and Dathan, Gilgamesh sought a greater truth, and found a companion to share his quest. The need for such a partner to provide balance and share the adventure is also a common mythological theme. Enkidu, who became that partner in this story, was a "wild man," the only one who was a match for the king. He was, however, fated to die, as is Dathan, so in this respect the myth enacted in the epic is more like the human variant than the Tamarian one. Unlike Dathan, however, Gilgamesh ultimately sought the truth for himself, for upon Enkidu's death mortality haunted the king and caused him to proceed on his quest alone. His search for immortality took him to strange, otherworldly locations in space and time, but in the end he was denied the actual goal of his quest, for man is fated to die. Like Dathan, however, he did achieve immortality of a kind, for each lives in perpetuity within the mythology of his species. And so it is that Picard can quote his story in the mythological twenty-fourth century within the twentieth-century myth of Star Trek. In the closing shot, gazing alone into space, Picard salutes Dathan using the Tamarian ritual gesture. It is a gesture that confirms the connection that has been forged between them, generated by a shared experience of living myth.

Like the probe that attaches itself to the *Enterprise* in "Masks," the Tamarian ship matches the capabilities of Starfleet's flagship in every respect and surpasses it in some. Apparently, belonging to a culture with a living mythological base does not preclude advanced technology, another challenge to currently held opinion in our culture. The beauty of this episode is that it treats mythology as a lived reality for people who fit our expectations of advanced societies, suggesting that in order to "connect" with such people we might want to review our dismissal of, or our demythologization of, our own tradition. The interface between the epic of Gilgamesh and the epic of Darmock and Gelad at Tenagra suggests that there is meaning to be found in such cultural and religious traditions and that the search for such meaning is important. Two characters, two cultures, two worlds may find in each other a source of shared community and experience, if only they can understand each other's stories.[3]

Traditionally, religions provide ways of understanding time and space and the nature of reality in the world as it is experienced. It might be argued that science has assumed this function in much of contemporary world culture. But we still respond *religiously* to the concepts presented to us by science. We *believe* that they are true. None of us has experienced the Big Bang; few of us have traveled in space to observe Earth from a distance and have the proof of our senses that the world is round. Watching the NASA Channel serves this function for some: One *believes* that the images on the TV screen are *real*. Ultimately, one believes these things to be true based on the authority attributed to their source, the testimony of the scientific community, the fact that images from those authoritative sources are duplicated in books, produced on film, displayed on our TV set and computer screens. These images and concepts shape perception and understanding, that is, "we accept the reality with which we are presented," to quote *The Truman Show*. One *knows* that Star Trek is science fiction and that the NASA Channel is science reality. But as the recent and hugely popular film *The Matrix* suggests, it is just possible that one is "living in a dream world." Science fiction and religious traditions share the proposition that there are alternate realities; perhaps the difference lies in who may have access to these, what purpose is served by accessing them, and what powers control them. Both forms require a leap of faith as the price of passage.

Time Warped:
The Geometry of Transformation

The final episode of *Star Trek: The Next Generation* ("All Good Things . . . ") forms a perfect frame (and a perfect circle) for the series when considered along with its very first episode, in which Q places humanity (in the form of Picard) on trial for its violence and hubris. The last episode places Picard in the position of saving humanity from an oblivion that he himself causes by trying to investigate it, a result of a judgment passed by the Q Continuum seven years later. Sequence, causality, and result are thrown into disarray in a plot as convoluted as a Möbius strip. "All Good Things . . ." also provides a compelling example of the *Enterprise* engaged, despite itself, in another perspective entirely. Here the concern is the message conveyed regarding the multiple nature of temporal reality and the presence of that message in the history of religions.

"All Good Things . . ." explores the conundrum of time. Might the future have an impact on the present or the past? Humanity has a fascination with time travel and an awareness of how dangerous such travel might prove to be by unhinging causality and changing sequences. Picard's disorientation and anxiety as he struggles with the experience of shifting through three separate time periods reveals some of the problematic implications of temporal theory. Q ridicules Picard for his "linear" thinking about time. Are there alternatives? He states: "What you were and what you are to become will always be with you." He suggests that we all carry our future selves inside of us, waiting to be revealed at the appropriate moment. The episode also suggests that there is such a thing as "antitime" and that its collision with "normal" time can cause a rupture in space. If this were truly the case, then space and time would be, in some sense, one and could be manipulated, as Q has obviously done here, and as the Traveler apparently did in earlier episodes. Q's suggestion that the mysteries of time and space as well as their resolution lie within ourselves, rather than "out there," takes its place among the best insights of religious traditions.

The closing image of the "All Good Things . . ." is circles: the circle of playing cards on the circular table in the circular saucer of the ship in the vastness of space, which may itself be circular, or spiraled, as the galaxy. The image of the circle/spiral is ubiquitous in Eastern religious imagery, from the Hindu and Buddhist mandalas, to the yin-yang symbol of the Tao, to the Shinto image of the rising sun; the circle emerges as the dominant manifestation of ultimate reality. It is ironic and interesting that at the end of the *Next Generation* series the predominant image is not linear at all but the persistent, spiritual image of the circle that also happens to form the letter Q.

What Price Illumination?
The Inner Light

"The Inner Light" is a favorite episode among Star Trek fans, one of many episodes that explore the possibility of alternate realities, parallel universes, and multiple lives. Suddenly connected to an alien probe, Captain Picard finds himself on an alien world (Kataan), as another person (Kamin), in another life. He apparently remains there well into old age, while only twenty-five minutes actually pass on the *Enterprise*, as his crew desperately seeks to revive him from a comatose state. The alternate reality presented here exists only within Picard, but it is no less real to him, or to the audience, than any in the *Next Generation* series. The central reality/illusion duality represents a matter of ultimate concern to both philosophy and religion. If the lines we draw between what is judged to be real and what is dismissed as illusion are largely culturally determined, what can we ultimately know about the nature of reality? This experience affects Picard profoundly, and its lasting emotional toll surfaces in other episodes, as does the flute he learns to play in the course of his life as Kamin. How can an experience not grounded in "reality" actually have such an impact? What *is* the inner light to which the title refers?

From the Eastern perspective, where reincarnation remains central to one's understanding of oneself and one's world, the long succession of one's lives may be understood as a form of *maya*. There are many stories of great sages in Indian tradition who by virtue of their wisdom and devotion are granted a glimpse into the ultimate nature of reality. The divine source and nature of maya determine that it is the only reality humans can know, but the limitations of human form and imagination are such that one may only experience a veiled and distorted reality. Hindu philosophy explains that human lives are constructed of layers of reality, influenced by perception and sensation, all of which are only relatively real. As long as one's accumulated karma—the residue of our deeds and under-standing—continues to be generated, one is bound to be re-born in order to strive to overcome it. Only then, in a break-through facilitated by the negation of ego or individual identity, might one have access to the truth that lies beyond this world of illusion, according to the sages of India. Picard's experience on Kataan parallels breakthrough tales that abound throughout many traditions, particularly in South Asia.[4]

How does the symbol of the flute function in this episode? As was true in "Masks," one artifact remains from the experi-ence and carries enormous meaning for the character who ac-quires it. Artifacts are invaluable tools in the attempt to under-stand other cultures, whether in archaeology, anthropology, or the study of religion. Like sacred texts, however, they cannot explain whole cultures. Picard's flute holds enormous meaning to him, triggering associations with those he loved. Musical in-struments often play a role in enabling trance states: the Greek god Pan used his flute to enable chaos and loss of control; the Hindu god Krishna plays his flute to call his worshippers, es-pecially the *gopi* cowgirls, to dance with him in devotional abandon. Without the role it played in Picard's life on Kataan, however, the flute would simply be an object.

Like the South Asian sage, Picard becomes almost the com-plete opposite of the self he (and we) knew—and totally se-duced by it. However alien this new life seems, it draws him inevitably closer until he embraces it, along with a wife, Eline. The distant, unemotional, career-oriented captain becomes a sensitive and caring family man, with a wife and children to whom he is completely devoted, on a planet that no longer exists. This total character reversal may be essential, in some way, to spiritual transformation. Like one who is reborn in Asian tradition, he carries with him certain inclinations toward behaviors and interests from his previous existence: astronomy, environmental science, and an approach to life characterized by practicality. As that former life fades in time and memory, these residues, like souvenirs, lose their power. When he is restored to his life on the *Enterprise*, it takes him some time to readjust, to become the person he was before. Later episodes confirm that he is permanently altered by this experience.[5]

The "inner light" suggests that his life as Kamin remains within him as a beacon in the darkness of his regular, normal existence, however satisfying he usually finds it to be. Even as Data emerges from his experience in "Masks" with the memories of an entire civilization within him, Picard carries his knowledge of Kataan and its inhabitants within him for the rest of his life. The inner experience is as powerful as any from the real world. This should, at least, raise questions regarding our understanding of experience, our interpretation of its meaning, and the nature of identity. Picard's life as Kamin is neither more nor less real than his life on the *Enterprise* or Patrick Stewart's "life" as Picard (cf. Chapter 2 and the discussion of "Ship in a Bottle"; after Professor Moriarty and the Countess have been safely captured in a capsule that will provide them with enough adventures for a virtual lifetime, Picard remarks, "Who knows, our reality may be very much like theirs, and all this might just be an elaborate simulation running inside a little device sitting on someone's table").

The proposition that there are alternate realities in space and time provides us options for imagining existence in a meaningful way, with underlying purposes, explanations of origins, ways of interpreting events and experiences, and a series of expectations regarding the future. In short, it provides imaginal options that parallel the goals of religious thought and practice. Contemporary Western culture rests uneasily between two perceived options. Either there is a guiding and reasonable force or presence that shapes the world—whether it is a deity in the traditional sense or a complex set of axioms or rules—or the universe is composed of random, unrelated chaos, meaningless and senseless.

The overarching mythos of Star Trek can be characterized as a resounding endorsement of progress, a conviction in the infinite and triumphant possibilities of science and technology, a confidence in the continuous and perfecting process of evolution. The fact that Star Trek is willing to question these assumptions and consider alternatives marks it as a sophisticated mythos. Its determination "to go where no one has gone before" places it squarely within the rubric of numerous heroic mythologies across human history and culture. When Q informs Picard in "All Good Things . . ." that the point of exploring space is to define "the unknown possibilities of existence," he invokes the generic definition of all spiritual quests. Star Trek really *does* want the best of both worlds—the secular humanistic confidence in the triumph of reason, and the emotional and transforming experience of myth. To achieve this goal, it is even willing to pair mythological content with ceremonial and transformative action and to consider them efficacious, that is to say, meaningful and useful.

Star Trek takes us on a journey into alternate realities in every episode. It invites its viewers to participate in the creative and compelling endeavor of mythmaking, in the search for meaning, and in the development of worldviews. It is not surprising, then, that it has inspired such an impassioned following. It not only represents or portrays many of religion's components, functions, and characteristics; it also uses them for inspiration. In modern America, that is enough to generate a considerable following. Such are the rules of engagement.

What Happens
When You Die?

Ross S. Kraemer

He's dead, Jim.

—Bones McCoy to Captain Kirk,
"The Enemy Within"

Star Trek's take on death and the afterlife suggests that what happens when you die might be relative if not personal. At the very least, Star Trek understands that different cultures have different ideas. Consistent with creator Gene Roddenberry's secular humanism, the fact that we die is crucial. As Captain Picard says to the immortality-seeking Doctor Tolian Soran in the film *Star Trek Generations* (the seventh in the series), "It's our mortality that defines us, Soran. It's part of the truth of our existence." Throughout Trek, how one lives this life is the question of consummate concern; questions about life after death are of much less interest. As on so many questions central to Terran religious traditions, Star Trek is ultimately agnostic about the answer to this one, as well.

Early Star Trek episodes paid virtually no attention to the fate of the dead. Although McCoy's line quickly became well known, death itself was of little interest. Once characters died, whether they were expendable ensigns or diabolical aliens, they were of no further concern to the crew of the *Enterprise*. In *Star Trek The Motion Picture* (the first film), however, the possibility of life after death receives extensive treatment. In this film, an ancient Earth probe (once known as *Voyager* 6, but now calling itself a corrupted form—V'Ger) attains consciousness during its wanderings through the universe and seeks to return to Earth to merge with "the Creator." To communicate with the *Enterprise* crew, V'Ger kills the character of Ilia (played by actress Persis Khambatta) and creates a replica of her form. To thwart the danger posed to Earth by V'Ger's desire to merge with its human creator, Kirk's successor, Captain Will Decker (played by a young Stephen Collins), volunteers to stand in as the Creator. In a final scene, Decker and the replicated Ilia, who had once been romantically involved, embrace in a quasimystical lightshow. Observing the fireworks, Kirk remarks that we may just have seen the creation of a new life-form. Decker was apparently killed in the merge, but he and Ilia were subsequently listed as missing in action.[1]

With *Star Trek II: The Wrath of Khan* and then *Star Trek III: The Search for Spock*, an explicit portrayal of the mystery of life after death emerges, along with the biblical theme of creation. In *Wrath of Khan*, the genetically enhanced Aka Khan Noonien Singh (played by Ricardo Montalban) avenges himself on Kirk and the *Enterprise*. Khan and his followers had been exiled to a remote, uninhabited planet years earlier, after Khan's failed attempt to take over the *Enterprise* in the Original Series episode "Space Seed" (aired February 1967). He steals an experimental device from the Regula I space station, a device created by Kirk's old lover Doctor Carol Marcus and her son (by Kirk), Doctor David Marcus. As Kirk reports on a tape stolen by Klingons, the so-called Genesis device was "life from lifelessness," designed to transform uninhabitable, sterile planets into living, breathing planets that were capable of sustaining whatever life-forms were delivered to it.

Khan is again foiled by Kirk and his crew, but at the cost of Spock's life, who sacrifices himself heroically. Khan has triggered a fatal reaction inside a radiation chamber. Knowing that no crew member could endure the lethal radiation doses, Spock locks himself inside the chamber, shutting down the reaction. He dies of radiation poisoning, separated from a grieving Kirk by protective walls. In a classic scene, the succumbing Spock presses his hand to Kirk's against the transparent partition and says, cryptically, "I have been, and always shall be, your friend. Live long and prosper."

Befittingly, Spock receives one of the most elaborate funerals ever witnessed on Star Trek. His body is consigned to a small pod marked with the insignia of the Federation. Dressed in formal uniforms, Kirk and the crew stand in two lines on either side of the pod while Kirk conducts a funeral service of sorts. A door is opened, and the pod is jettisoned. It comes to rest on the newly formed planet Genesis, created when Khan prematurely triggered the Genesis device.

The next film, *Search for Spock*, then became Star Trek's first and most obvious exploration of Christian themes of sacrificial, salvific death and resurrection. At the conclusion of *Wrath of Khan*, Spock dies a sacrificial death in which the life of the one is intentionally offered to save the lives of the many. The dying Spock, in his death chamber, consoles the anguished Kirk:

> Spock: It's logical. The needs of the many outweigh . . .
> Kirk: . . . the needs of the few . . .
> Spock: . . . or the one.

In *Search for Spock*, through a complex plot that interweaves allusions to ancient Terran creation narratives, Christian mythic themes, and Vulcan beliefs about death and the soul, Spock's *katra* (soul) is united with his cloned body, which has regenerated on the planet's surface. Shortly after the *Enterprise* arrives back at Starfleet headquarters in San Francisco, the crew detects a life-form in Spock's supposedly sealed quarters. Investigating, Kirk finds Doctor McCoy in some distress.

> McCoy: Jim, help me. You left me on Genesis. Why did you do
>   that? Help me, Jim, take me home. . .
> Kirk: We are home. . . .
> McCoy: Then it's not too late. Climb the steps of Mount Seleya.

The usually perceptive Kirk doesn't seem to realize that it's not McCoy who's speaking but rather Spock; he counters that Mount Seleya is found on Vulcan. The doctor's odd behavior becomes comprehensible only after Spock's father, Ambassador Sarek, comes to Kirk, seeking to learn the fate of Spock's *katra*. Dismissing Kirk's attempts to offer him condolences, Sarek asks brusquely why Kirk left Spock on Genesis.

> Sarek: Spock trusted you and you denied him his future.
> Kirk: I saw no future. . . .

> Sarek: Only his body was in death, Kirk, and you were the last one to be with him. . . . He entrusted you with his very essence—with everything that was not of the body. He asked you to bring him to us, and to bring that which he gave you, his *katra*, his living spirit.

When Kirk claims he knows nothing of this, Sarek mind-melds with him, concluding that Spock did not, in fact, entrust his *katra* to Kirk. Once Kirk reruns the conveniently available tapes of Spock's final moments, it becomes clear that Spock had, instead, entrusted his *katra* to McCoy just before entering the radiation chamber. Sarek tells Kirk that he must bring the suffering McCoy and the body of Spock to Mount Seleya, where both will find peace—although how, he doesn't say.

The Search for Spock broke new ground in several ways. First, it offered audiences a tutorial on esoteric Vulcan religious beliefs and practices. We learn that the *katra* appears to be the Vulcan concept of the soul, the living spirit. We also learn that the *katra* is substantial enough that Vulcans dying far from home can transfer it, by means of a mind-meld, to someone who can then return the *katra* back to Vulcan, where, apparently, it is then stored in some fashion.

Sarek is noncommittal regarding the fate of Spock's body and the *katra* retrieved from McCoy. He expects that Kirk and his crew will retrieve Spock's lifeless body and return it to Vulcan. The possibilities become more complex when a young, but rapidly aging, Spock is found on the surface of the planet. In a scene rich with biblical allusions, both verbal and visual, David Marcus and a Vulcan lieutenant named Saavik beam down to the planet to check out a life-form reading emanating from the vicinity of Spock's burial tube. At first they find only a swarming mass of slimy creatures that David quickly recognizes as microbes on the surface of the tube; they have quickly evolved due to the unusual conditions on Genesis ("They became fruitful and multiplied," David says). He then opens the tube, which contains only a garment, not the body of Spock. Given the brevity of this scene, many viewers can miss the parallel to the Gospel of John (20:3–9), where Jesus' disciples find not only an empty tomb but the cloths in which the body of Jesus had been wrapped (see also the Gospel of Luke 24:12); together they point to the bodily resurrection of Jesus. In *Search for Spock*, the empty tube and Spock's burial robe hint of resurrection and his imminent appearance in the flesh. The sudden sound of a voice crying out in some distress offers additional affirmation. (Star Trek writers reuse these images in a *Voyager* TV episode; see discussion below.)

After a conflict with Klingons that leads to the death of Kirk's son David, the fully regenerated adult Spock is brought back to Vulcan; Sarek asks for the performance of an ancient Vulcan rite, *fal-tor-pan*, the refusion of the *katra* with the body. This rite, which had been performed in ages long past, ultimately succeeds to the relief of fans. One of Star Trek's most popular characters, Mr. Spock, has been resurrected.

The Vulcan beliefs and practices revealed in *Search for Spock* are interesting for many students of religion. We finally see a culture that clearly believes in distinctly separate elements of being: Despite the physical body that is finite and subject to death and disintegration, a "spiritual essence" of some sort that is distinct from the body can be separated in the event of impending death, capable of continuing existence apart from the body. We also see the "truth" of the beliefs of Vulcan culture, for Spock most certainly does have a *katra*. When Kirk reruns the tapes of Spock's final moments, we see Spock undertake a split-second mind-meld with the unaware McCoy and utter the word "remember." Then, during the ancient Vulcan ceremony, we see McCoy yield up the *katra* and watch the effect of its transference into the regenerated Spock. Nimoy, dressed in a white garment that looks like a monk's robe made of terry cloth, repeats to a tremulous Kirk his farewell speech *from Wrath of Khan* (including the crucial cryptic line, "I have been, and always shall be, your friend"); we know that his restoration is complete. The cloned, soulless body has become the true Spock, his essence having been restored to a genetically identical copy of his sacrificed corpse.

For the first time, then, Star Trek offers a vision of the resurrection of the body, in the process affirming that such things are not only the substance of untestable belief but also of ordinary galactic reality, at least on Vulcan. *Search for Spock* may not tell us what happens when *we* die, but it certainly tells us what happens when ordinary Vulcans die (or an extraordinary half-Vulcan, half-human under extraordinary circumstances in an extraordinary place).[2] Conveniently, the instability of the Genesis Project destroys the planet of Spock's regeneration, guaranteeing that his resurrection will not soon be repeated by others.

The TV series *Star Trek: The Next Generation* began to address questions about God and religion generally; thereafter questions about death received subtler exploration. In "Where Silence Has Lease" (*Next Generation*, aired November 1988), an alien named Nagilum threatens to kill a substantial percentage of the *Enterprise* crew to satisfy its desire to comprehend human understandings of life and death. The writers used the episode to set forth and comment on competing Terran conceptions, from the mouth of Picard:

Some see [death] as a changing into an indestructible form
. . . forever unchanging. They believe that the purpose of the
entire universe is to then maintain that form in an Earthlike
garden which will give delight and pleasure through all eternity.
On the other hand there are those who hold to the idea of our
blinking into nothingness with all of our experiences and hopes
and dreams merely a delusion.

Commandeering the body of Data, Nagilum asks Picard to
take a position. His ultimately vague and imprecise reply
might be taken as a fair representation of the humanist views
of Gene Roddenberry and, by implication, of the entire series:

Considering the marvelous complexity of the universe, its
clockwork perfection, its balance of this against that . . . matter,
energy, gravitation, time, dimension, I believe that our existence
must be more than either of these philosophies, that what we
are goes beyond Euclidean or other "practical" measuring systems . . . and that our existence is part of a reality beyond what
we understand now as reality.

Many later episodes explore (if not exploit) the question of
resurrection in the flesh. The bodily resurrection of savior figures is a theme taken up again in Next Generation, in an important episode ("Rightful Heir," May 1993) about a legendary
Klingon warrior-king, Kahless the Unforgettable. According to
Klingon lore, Kahless had once united warring Klingon factions and had promised to return someday. Venerated by later
generations of Klingons, Kahless was the focus of extensive
devotion and millenarian fervor, including by the Guardians at
a monastery on Boreth, where they awaited his return from
Sto-Vo-Kor, the realm of the Klingon righteous (warrior) dead.

At the opening of "Rightful Heir," the *Enterprise*'s Klingon security chief, Lieutenant Worf, has been trying to use traditional Klingon rites (which parallel Terran practices) to summon a vision of Kahless. His lack of success provokes a crisis of faith in Worf, who not only doubts the truth of Klingon belief in Kahless but also wonders whether he ever truly believed in the first place. Granted a leave by Picard to pursue his spiritual quest, Worf travels to Boreth in a scene that evokes the Christian canonical gospels: Worf is the first to encounter the "risen" (actually cloned) Kahless; like the famous disciple Thomas in the Gospel of John (20:24–29), he doubts that the person he sees is truly resurrected.

Eventually, the Klingon leader Gowron, himself skeptical that the man could be Kahless and convinced that such beliefs are dangerous, proposes to test Kahless against a sample of the original Kahless's blood preserved on an ancient knife. When the blood matches, Worf concedes. Despite his earlier statement that belief in Kahless's identity is not a matter of empirical evidence, it is precisely such seemingly hard empirical evidence that resolves his doubt.

Convinced that he is now in the presence of the true and returned Kahless, Worf seeks answers about Sto-Vo-Kor and life after death. But Kahless demurs: He claims that he is merely a traveler and that in his present form he knows only this world, nothing of the next. Instead, Kahless tells Worf that it was Worf's own purity of heart that summoned Kahless back from the dead, and he invites Worf to stay at his side as he restores the unity of the Klingon Empire.

Ultimately, of course, it turns out that Kahless is not exactly the returned warrior but a clone, created by the Guardians, who have implanted within him memories of the Klingon scriptures, so that he truly believes himself to be the revived

Kahless. Horrified at this discovery, Worf tells the Guardians that the Klingons do not need a false god. They counter that who can say whether or not the prophecy of Kahless's return was meant to be fulfilled in precisely this way?

Many modern studies have shown that humans respond to serious apparent disconfirmation of cherished beliefs in various ways; in "Rightful Heir," Klingons would appear to do the same. Despite strong evidence that Kahless is merely a clone, some Klingons continued to believe he has returned as the messiah. When questioned by Data, Worf responds that he does not believe in this Kahless but does not know whether he still believes in the eventual coming of Kahless. To this confession, Data acknowledges that he, too, has trouble with what Western social scientists often call "cognitive dissonance" (what we feel when our expectations and our experiences don't mesh): Despite the evidence that Data is not human, he persists in believing that he is a person. In the minds of the people, says Worf, Kahless is still powerful, even if he's a clone. People believe despite the facts and will, in this case, engage in civil war if Gowron opposes Kahless. Worf proposes a peaceful solution: Since Klingons have, in fact, become decadent and corrupt, the cloned Kahless can provide moral leadership—he is, according to Worf, the "rightful heir" of the original Kahless. Kahless offers cooperation to Gowron, who then kneels before Kahless.

In the final scene, Worf tells Kahless that he went to Boreth to find his faith but no longer knows what to believe. Kahless comforts him with the observation that if Kahless's words are true, what does it matter if he returns—the words are more important than the man. As he takes his leave, Worf acknowledges the truth of this view when he salutes the clone with the Klingon farewell, "*Kaplach*, Kahless."

"Rightful Heir" is one of Star Trek's most transparent takes on Christian beliefs in the bodily resurrection of the messianic Jesus. It offers at least a mild critique of those who continue to believe in the face of irrefutable evidence to the contrary, yet it resists any facile rejection of Christianity. The final scene between Kahless and Worf could easily stand as the episode's ultimate stance on the issues it raises: If the moral teachings of Kahless (and, by analogy, other messianic teachers) are true, what difference does it make whether they return or not?

More important, "Rightful Heir" offers a complex portrait of Klingon beliefs about death and the afterlife. We learn that Klingons believe strongly in the existence of life after death, in physical locations where the dead continue to exist in some kind of continuity with earlier incarnations. The righteous warrior dead live on in a place called Sto-Vo-Kor, reminiscent of Valhalla in ancient Germanic religion. Located in Asgard, home of the gods, Valhalla was traditionally the hall established by the main deity, Odin, for slain heroes, where they fought by day and feasted by night. This parallel is hardly surprising, given the similarities of Klingon culture to the Vikings and Norse generally. Disgraced Klingon warriors instead go to a place of suffering and disrepute known as Gre'thor, guarded by a mythic figure named Fek'lhr.

Although Gre'thor is only occasionally mentioned in *Next Generation*, a much later episode in *Voyager* ("Barge of the Dead," aired October 1999) offers a detailed picture of Gre'thor. Chief engineer B'Elanna Torres has a visionary experience in which her rejection of Klingon practices and beliefs condemns her mother to a dishonorable eternity in Gre'thor. To rescue her mother, B'Elanna must enter Gre'thor herself and redeem the family honor. The title of the episode is drawn from the Klingon belief that the dead travel to Gre'thor on a barge steered by a ferryman. In Norse mythology, Asgard was entered by crossing a rainbow bridge called Bifrost, guarded by Heimdall, the watchman of the gods. Most Star Trek viewers are likely to see Gre'thor as incorporating ancient Greek beliefs about Charon the ferryman, who carried the dead across the River Styx in exchange for a coin (placed in the mouth of the dead in actual ancient practice), as well as widespread Terran ideas about the retributive suffering of the dead in hot and unpleasant realms.

Unlike *Search for Spock*, "Rightful Heir" and other episodes that portray Klingon beliefs in the afterlife never prove the "truth" of such beliefs, even if only for what happens when Klingons die. When Worf's Trill wife, Jadzia Dax, dies on *Deep Space Nine*, he engages in a lengthy Klingon rite to transfer her soul to Sto-Vo-Kor, but whether Worf's performance truly installs Jadzia's soul there cannot be determined. Likewise, in "Barge of the Dead" B'Elanna's efforts to transfer her mother from Gre'thor to Sto-Vo-Kor take place in a dreamlike state that may or may not be understood to have actually occurred. In *Search for Spock*, the regenerated, if not resurrected, Spock *is* who he seems to be. Like Kahless, his body is cloned, but whereas Kahless possesses only implanted artificial memories, Spock possesses his original *katra*. Whether they can die again is not clear, but their resurrections differ from that of Jesus; having overcome death, Jesus does not die again.

Star Trek's most detailed and fascinating exploration of the afterlife and resurrection appear in "Emanations" (*Voyager*, aired March 1995). In search of a newly discovered, highly useful element, an away team beams inside an asteroid, where they soon discover eighteen dead humanoid bodies shrouded in a biopolymer of undetermined nature. Some away team members wish to scan the bodies, but Commander Chakotay refuses, believing the asteroid to be a burial ground whose sacrality should not be violated by unnecessary scientific exploration (alluding to Chakotay's Native American ancestral traditions). The crew observes the bodies visually and begins to debate their conclusions when interrupted by the formation of something called a subspace vacule. Chakotay and Torres are beamed safely back to *Voyager*, but Ensign Harry Kim disappears, and in his place is another shrouded, newly dead female, who is revived by the Doctor (*Voyager's* anonymous medical hologram) and cured of her mortal illness.

Meanwhile, on the surface of an unknown planet, a group of aliens gather around an object they call a cenotaph (from the Greek word *kenotaphion*, meaning an empty tomb; its significance becomes apparent later), conducting a death ritual for a female member of their community named Ptera. Shouts from within the cenotaph interrupt the ritual, which we soon find is called a "transference ceremony." Opening the vessel, the celebrants find Harry Kim. These beings are the Vhnori, and they believe that after death they travel, embodied, to the Next Emanation, where they are reunited with deceased loved ones. The Vhnori who discover Kim surmise that he has come from the Next Emanation and send for the thanatologist, a death expert.

While awaiting the thanatologist Kim engages in a seemingly casual conversation with Hakil Garan, a man who is about to die. Unaware he is about to introduce chaos to this culture, Kim tells Hakil that the last thing he remembers was conducting research on an asteroid, where he and his crewmates found some dead bodies. Hakil expresses distress and amazement at the mention of dead people, but before the conversation can continue the thanatologist arrives. When Hakil interjects Kim's mention of corpses, the thanatologist asks to see Harry in private.

It turns out that neither the Vhnori nor Kim has an accurate sense of the relationship between their respective worlds, or perhaps even their universes. In response to Kim's questioning, the thanatologist insists that where Harry is now is the place of the living—where he came from was another dimension—the afterlife, the Next Emanation. Such an explanation accords with Vhnori cosmology but not with Kim's, and much of the plot revolves around Kim's attempt to return home in the face of Vhnori resistance.

Meanwhile, back on *Voyager* the revived Ptera wakes to find herself not in the Next Emanation but on a Federation starship, a reality she has difficulty comprehending. When she learns that the subspace vacules deposit what appear to be dead Vhnoris inside the asteroids about every two hours, Ptera is confronted with devastating falsification of Vhnori beliefs. Deeply distressed, she begs the crew to find a way to send her home. Their risky attempt, described in classic Star Trek vernacular, fails, and Ptera dies again—this time for good. Captain Kathryn Janeway sends her body down to the asteroid, where "she was meant to be."

Kim's presence on the Vhnori planet creates similar challenges. In a lengthy conversation with Hakil Garan, the same conflicts are aired—cultural beliefs versus bodily evidence. Hakil shares Ptera's horror at the thought that Vhnori dead simply decay on some unknown asteroid. Through classic trickery, Harry manages to escape from the Vhnori and return to *Voyager*, changing places with Hakil just before the transference ceremony and allowing the doubting Hakil to live the rest of his life with trustworthy friends in the mountains, leaving his family content in their beliefs that he has traveled to the Next Emanation.[3]

The nature of life after death is explored in a key scene in which Ptera tells Kes (*Voyager's* Ocampa crew member, taken aboard in the first episode) that the Vhnori were always told that they would see beautiful sights in the Next Emanation, with new eyes. Not unlike those puzzled persons who appear to be reflected in Paul's correspondence, Ptera wonders whether all the people who die on her world end up as lifeless corpses. Kes replies that when people die on her world they bury them beneath the soil and believe that their souls or spirits are released into the afterlife. Her Ocampa people call this essence *komra*, and Kes suggests that maybe something similar happens to the Vhnoris. But Ptera responds emphatically that the Vhnoris don't believe in a spirit—they believe that when they die they reappear as physical beings with arms and legs. They travel on to the Next Emanation as themselves and are reunited with their families. Ptera's enormous distress at discovering otherwise is devastating.

A similar conversation occurs on the planet between Harry and Hakil. Like Kes, Harry attempts to reconcile Vhnori beliefs with the bodies on the asteroid using a similar explanation: Perhaps what he saw after all were the corporeal remains of the Vhnori, and they do go on to a higher level of existence. Like Ptera, Hakil is unconvinced and expresses his anxiety that perhaps when we die we simply cease to exist. Harry is only able to respond that he has no answers—either for the fate of the Vhnori or the fate of his own people.

In the final scene, between Janeway and Kim, we see a convenient recap of the dilemma: Kim reflects that the Vhnori think they know what happens after death, and that they look forward to it, are prepared for it. Yet the truth is that they are wrong; they don't have an afterlife. They simply die and then decay inside those asteroids. Janeway tells him not to be so sure—that she has observed their bodies release a neural energy that becomes part of the ambient electromagnetic field surrounding the planet—energy that is unusually dynamic, varied in pattern complexity and quantum density. Harry asks whether she is saying that they do have an afterlife, that the energy field is the place where they do exist at a higher level of consciousness, as they believe. Janeway concedes that she isn't certain—that what we don't know about death is far greater than what we do know.[4]

And even though "Emanations" undercuts beliefs in bodily resurrection, it attempts to mediate between the Vhnori belief in resurrection and the unnerving evidence. Janeway's explanation in her final conversation with Harry Kim is plausible, and it offers a scientific underpinning for religious belief. Talk of "neural energy" and "ambient radiation" may suggest some continuing existence, just not in the form believed by the Vhnoris. Only the resurrection of the physical body is demonstrably false.

Yet in a subtle irony, Harry Kim's only chance to return to his own reality is to die and hope that the *Voyager* crew will be able to resurrect him before his death is irrevocable. Thus, despite the show's insistence that the dead are not resurrected in a physical body, Harry Kim does indeed die and experience resurrection. (Although Ptera, too, experiences resurrection in the body, her experience is wholly unsatisfactory, and she expresses the willingness to die again, rather than endure this particular form of resurrection among strangers.)

Star Trek's representation of what happens when you die intertwines with that of another central concern in Terran religions: Are we simply material beings, or is some aspect of our being separable from our bodies, capable of existing prior to birth and after death?

In Western monotheist traditions, it is common to approach the issue as the existence of a soul and the relationship of the body to the soul. But Terran beliefs vary considerably; in some traditions the soul is the spark of breathy life that animates the body and departs at death with the final exhalation. In others, the soul is the innermost self, the true personality that can be strengthened by doing good but becomes weakened through evil deeds. Souls can be viewed as divine, a part of God or of a fallen god imprisoned in a fleshly dungeon, longing to escape back to heavenly realms. In still other views, the soul is a bit of the universal Soul, which is selfless and without personality, so that at liberation it simply merges back into the impersonal All. In still other traditions, such as Buddhism, there is no permanent, constant, eternal soul.

Beliefs about the fate of the soul after death also vary. Ancient Greeks and Israelites believed that all persons, regardless of their deeds on Earth, shared a common fate: Their bodies disintegrated while their souls descended into a shadowy netherworld (Hades in Greek, She'ol in Hebrew). Later, many Jews and Christians came to believe that the soul would be punished or rewarded after death for the deeds of the ensouled body. Some ancient Greek philosophers believed, as do modern Hindus and many others, that the souls of the dead were reincarnated in other bodies, depending on how they lived in their previous lives. Some do not believe in the existence of the soul. A scientific materialist view holds that everything can be explained through science and that there is no evidence for any soul at all. The soul thus becomes a metaphor.

Star Trek III: The Search for Spock posits that the Vulcan *katra* is real, material enough to be stashed in the unwitting McCoy before Spock enters his death chamber. But when Captain Kirk seeks permission to take a Starfleet vessel to Genesis to retrieve Spock's body, the superior officer says, "Honestly, I never understood Vulcan mysticism." Kirk replies, "You don't have to believe—I'm not even sure that I believe. But if there's even a chance Spock has an eternal soul, then it's my responsibility . . . as surely as if it were my very own." Yet the fact that Vulcans possess a *katra* does not mean that everyone in the universe does. A *Next Generation* episode explains that the physical similarities of Romulans, Terrans, Klingons, Vulcans, and others are due to ancient common ancestry in a race that had seeded the galaxy with its DNA, but not everyone genetically related to Vulcans appears to have a *katra* (see "The Chase," aired April 1993).

Nothing suggests that Terrans have a *katra*, although Kes's Ocampa people believe that they have a *komra* that separates from the physical body at death. Whether Terrans have souls receives a somewhat contradictory treatment in *Search for Spock*. Despite Kirk's skepticism, toward the end of the film, when Sarek thanks Kirk having saved Spock at the cost of his own son David, Kirk replies, "What I have done, I had to do. . . . If I hadn't tried, the cost would have been my soul."

Many scholars, including religionists, anthropologists, and others, have observed that beliefs about the existence of a soul—and those about the relationship of the body and that soul—are closely related to other aspects of human culture—social, political, economic, and so on. For instance, those who believe that the soul is distinct, separable from the body, the true pure being that is superior to the corporeal vessel, are likely to have distinct views about the physical body. Those who believe that there is no aspect of the self apart from the physical body, and those who believe that to be human is to be an embodied soul, will view things differently. Aspects of ordinary life—self-discipline, desire, judgment of others, social welfare, public health, ecology—may indeed be affected by their belief in taking care of the individual soul. The same people may believe that the soul merits from concern for the poor and the suffering of others, yet others may be more willing to wage war and die in service, believing their soul will continue to exist.

Such views can be related to ideas about gender: Persons and communities who elevate the soul over the body often associate the body with women, with the feminine; the soul is associated with men, with the masculine. We do not argue a causal relationship here; we simply point out that sets of religious beliefs often come in packages: One set of beliefs can correlate with others. In fact, a pronounced dualism with regard to body and soul is often one part of a system that envisions the universe as governed by two opposing principles, one good, the other evil. In such systems hierarchical dualisms are perceived in many (if not all) facets of human existence: Individuals, practices, and other aspects of life are either good or they are evil. Such dualism is frequently expressed in pairs of binary oppositions: light and dark, right and left, heaven and Earth, rationality and irrationality, asceticism and sexuality, culture and nature, male and female, the spiritual (the soul) and the physical (the body).

Surprisingly, the writers of Star Trek do not overtly make these connections. They portray cultures with fairly pronounced beliefs about the separation of body and soul, but they do not seem concerned about demonstrating how such beliefs correlate with aspects of social experience and thought. The Klingons, for instance, believe in the separation of the soul from the body at death and rank the soul above the body, but there appears to be no Klingon myth of the fall of the soul. The Klingon hunter-warrior ethos is predominantly male in its orientation, although Klingon women can be warriors. Male kinship and lineage remain crucial, and the few Klingon women leaders we see are unsympathetic characters. Klingons have a gendered hierarchy.

Vulcans also believe in the separation of body and soul, and their ascetic practices, including monasticism, suggest a devaluing of the body relative to the spirit that is more consistent with early representations of Vulcan gender arrangements. Recall the willingness of T'Pring in "Amok Time" (Original Series, aired September 1967) "to become the property of the victor" in the rite of *koon-ut-kal-if-fee* (loosely translated as "marriage or challenge"), then compare subsequent series, in which Vulcans are depicted as less sexist and more egalitarian. This may be a function of the show's increasing move to portray its favorite cultures as egalitarian, not an overt attempt to plumb the subtle connections between beliefs and social experience.

Likewise, Ferengi believe in the separation of the body and the soul. They have pronounced gender differences and valuations—almost a parody of a sexist system, consistent with their general depiction as comic relief. Numerous episodes mock the Ferengi for such customs as forbidding women to wear clothing in public and for excluding women from pursuing profit (the most valued Ferengi activity). Bajorans seem to have a fairly egalitarian system, with women playing integral parts in economic, political, and religious systems. Bajoran beliefs about the nature of death and the fate of the dead remain enigmatic, but they believe in the existence of something called the *pagh*, a person's life-force, from which one gains strength and courage. Like the Vulcan *katra*, the *pagh* can be observed or perceived by others. In the inaugural episode of *Deep Space Nine*, the Bajoran religious leader Kai Opaka insists on reading Sisko's *pagh* (grabbing his ear forcefully and focusing attentively). And in the *Next Generation* episode "The Next Phase" (aired May 1992), we learn that Bajoran religion includes a belief in spirits of the dead, called *borads*.

Beliefs about the afterlife are also often closely related to beliefs about how to live in this life. People who believe they will be judged after death on the basis of their actions in this life may well make choices intended to guarantee them rewards. If one does not believe in future judgment, then constraints might be imposed by internalized cultural values and by practical consequences of one's actions. Yet many people are capable of subscribing to a set of beliefs that are not put into practice during daily existence. Beliefs about human frailty and divine forgiveness are often important here, allowing people to understand that less-than-ideal choices are part of human weakness, which does not preclude blessed immortality. Likewise, beliefs about reincarnation allow people to anticipate release from embodied existence proportionate to their spiritual successes.

In Star Trek, some galactic cultures believe in postmortem retribution. Klingons believe that the honorable dead reside happily in Sto-Vo-Kor; the dishonored suffer in Gre'thor. In the *Voyager* episode "Barge of the Dead," we see that actions can bring dishonor to others (at least family members) and cause that person to dwell (at least temporarily) in Gre'thor. In this episode, it appears that the converse is true; when B'Elanna redeems her honor (by descending into "hell"), her mother is released from Gre'thor and installed in Sto-Vo-Kor.

Ferengi beliefs about retributive justice illuminate the connections religionists see between cultural structures and religious beliefs. Their most cherished cultural values—business and profit—are believed to be divinely authorized and promulgated (perhaps by a god) in a set of laws known as the 285 Rules of Acquisition. Those who live according to the 285 Rules will receive reward (or retribution) in an afterworld—the Divine Treasury. Ferengi death rites make it clear that the Ferengi must also believe in some soul that survives death, for the bodies of the Ferengi are immediately cremated, their remains sold at auction. In yet another instance of the pervasive importance of a profit economy for Ferengi values, the prices paid for the cremains are taken as an indication of the prestige of the deceased, prestige that itself depends on how well the deceased fulfilled the 285 Rules.

Ferengi religion seems almost a parody, perhaps of traditional Judaism. The 285 Rules evoke Judaism's 613 Commandments. Ferengi prohibition against women engaging in business is reminiscent of traditional exclusion of women from Judaism's most culturally valued activity—the study of Torah. (We are left to wonder whether Ferengi women are excluded from the afterlife and the postmortem rituals.) Both traditions prohibit autopsy, although Ferengi cremation suggests the prohibition is not over concern for the integrity of the body or related to beliefs about bodily resurrection. Critics have pointed out a disturbing correlation between Ferengi attributes (love of profit that overrides communal decency; the large, sexualized head feature, in this case ears) and negative Jewish stereotypes. Regardless of the truth of this critique, Ferengi religion, and beliefs about retributive justice after death, illustrate the correspondence in Terran cultures between the structures of particular societies and the content and forms of their religious beliefs.

Ferengi beliefs in the afterlife (and Klingon beliefs to a lesser degree) illustrate the notion that Terrans often envision the universe in two realms, generally but not absolutely separate, whose characteristics tend to be binary opposites. One realm (the world of ordinary experience) is characterized by mortality, powerlessness, suffering, and the absence of the divine; the other realm (often, but not always, imagined as accessible only after death) is characterized by immortality, power, lack of suffering, and the presence of the divine. Grafted upon these oppositions are other binary oppositions (female and male, evil and good, death and life, soul and body, etc.). This second realm is often portrayed as the opposite of how life is experienced in this world—at least as to the negative aspects of life in this world. It is also typically imaged in terms of central, or root, cultural metaphors. For the Ferengi, the Divine Treasury is a more perfect, permanent version of the profit-driven realm they presently inhabit; as for Klingons, honor and dishonor, the warrior ethos and the hunter ethos, are given eternal validation in Sto-Vo-Kor and Gre'thor.

For Starfleet personnel, however, there is little belief in an afterlife. Time after time, the consequences of actions in *this life* matter most. Accordingly, even if there were some form of existence after death, it has little bearing on crucial questions now. Such is life on a Federation starship. This is illustrated in the 1994 film *Star Trek Generations*. Traditions about heaven common to Judaism, Christianity, and Islam are explored, and largely rejected, in this film. Central to the plot is a place known as the Nexus, outside ordinary time and experience. There, people experience only pleasure in the form of gratification of cherished desire. Thought and experience are seamless. Those who have experienced the Nexus, and left, are forever bereft, forever desirous of returning. It is Paradise and Paradise Lost.

But *Generations* adroitly sidesteps the question of life after death. Those in the Nexus aren't dead, whether Guinan, or

Picard, or even James T. Kirk, who, it turns out, didn't really die in 2293; instead, he was caught up in the passing Nexus in the nick of time as he was cast into space, and he has spent the intervening seventy-eight years in bliss (including blissful ignorance of this truth). The Nexus may be akin to Paradise, but when Kirk does finally die at the climax of *Generations*, he has (indeed must have) left the Nexus.

In *Generations*, the perpetual pleasure of the Nexus is shown to be antithetical to authentic existence. Because there is no death, life there could have no meaning. No matter how happy he had been, Kirk agrees with Picard that it is preferable to leave the Nexus and die a meaningful death rather than remain and never experience death. For Kirk, the ultimate meaning of life is found when he dies while preventing Tolian Soran from destroying the nourishing star of a major planetary system as part of his plan to alter the course of the Nexus so he may jump aboard at just the right moment. Picard's retort to Soran, which we quoted near the beginning of this chapter, is definitive: "It's our mortality that defines us." Life without death, even life in Paradise, is not truly life. Life after death, even in Paradise, is not nearly as interesting to contemplate as life in the face of death.

We should make some final observations about what happens when you die in the Star Trek universe. The dead are usually unable to contact the living, and as for ghosts, several episodes debunk that possibility through scientific explanation. In the *Next Generation* episode "The Next Phase" (aired May 1992), Geordi La Forge and the engaging Bajoran character Ensign Ro Laren apparently die in a transporter accident, then wander the *Enterprise* in a ghostlike state. After the accident they are unable to communicate with any of the *Enterprise* crew, although they can see and hear the others just fine. They also find themselves able to pass through walls and other physical barriers. Whereas Geordi is sure their condition has a scientific explanation and that they are, in fact, alive and well, Ro is increasingly convinced they are dead, a conviction supported when she witnesses Doctor Beverly Crusher filling out their death certificates on the computer. The probability that she is now dead—and a ghost to boot—dismays Ro. She tells Geordi that when she was a child she thought Bajoran beliefs in *borads* were just superstitions. Now, it seems to her, those superstitions might have been right. Unsurprisingly, however, it is Geordi who turns out to be right.

Next Generation debunked another ghost story in an episode entitled "Sub Rosa" (aired January 1994). After Beverly Crusher's grandmother dies, she finds a diary in which her grandmother describes an affair with a dashing young lover. Like the genie in Aladdin's lamp, this lover appears to Beverly in the form of a ghost when she lights one of her grandmother's candles. Beverly, too, is drawn to the man, named Ronin, with whom she has a brief passionate, gratifying affair. The liaison becomes dangerous when Ronin attempts to persuade Beverly to leave the *Enterprise* and stay with him.

Although Beverly's family lore had considered Ronin a ghost in the usual Western tradition, it turns out that he, too, has a perfectly ordinary scientific materialist explanation. Ronin is just another peculiar life-form, an anaphasic plasma being who had used the women of Beverly's family to experience corporeality. When Beverly destroys her grandmother's candle, she destroys Ronin as well. In "Sub Rosa," Terran beliefs about ghosts turn out to be grounded in real experiences misunderstood for lack of adequate knowledge; as in "Who Mourns for Adonais?" from the Original Series, ancient beliefs in Apollo and the other gods were grounded in real experiences of beings whom Greeks could not properly identify.

Voyager tackled the issue of ghosts from the same perspective. In one episode ("Coda," January 29, 1997), a critically injured Janeway seems to encounter the ghost of her father, who turns out to be a ghoulish but very much alive alien who feeds off the energy of dying people—but needs their assent to do so. The alien has ransacked Janeway's memories for the image of her father, hoping to trick her into assenting to her consumption.

In Star Trek, then, the dead pose no threat to the living. Sufficient threats are provided by any number of living beings.

Star Trek has thus demonstrated more interest in exploring transformations of existence. Indeed, the entire *Next Generation* series could be read as an exploration of human potential for transformation into something as yet unknown, something that may, in fact, verge on the divine. Periodically, one character or another transforms into a very different kind of being, one whose form and experience are almost, but not completely, incomprehensible at present. In *Next Generation*, it was the human Wesley Crusher who, under the tutelage of the Traveler, learned to use his own inner powers to stop time and, ultimately, to transcend the limitations of the human body and the boundaries between time, thought, matter, and energy. At the conclusion of "Journey's End" in the final season of *Next Generation*, Wesley leaves his mother and the *Enterprise* crew and departs with the Traveler to further realize his potential. In "Transfigurations" (aired June 1990), the mysterious Christlike figure known only as John Doe is in the process of transforming from a corporeal humanoid life-form into a noncorporeal energy being. (The title may allude to the transfiguration of Jesus into a being whose face shines like the sun

[Matt. 17: 2] and whose garments are intensely white.) Forced to become a fugitive from his own people, who are frightened by a process they do not as yet comprehend, Doe is rescued by Doctor Crusher and the *Enterprise*, who protect him and observe his transfiguration. In *Voyager*, it is the Ocampa Kes who metamorphosizes into a being of light, no longer bound by the confines of time and space, and leaves the ship and its crew for a new form of existence. At the conclusion of the *Deep Space Nine* series another human, Benjamin Sisko, finds himself transported to the company of the noncorporeal, nonlinear Prophets. Although the show is ambiguous about Sisko's fate, it seems clear that he is not dead and probably has become like the Prophets. Appearing to his simultaneously grieving and relieved wife, Kasidy Yates, in a visionary form much like that in which the Prophets have previously appeared to him, he promises her that he will return at some point. Since, however, he now knows that his own life is not linear (he is, after all, truly the emissary of the Prophets and the son of a Bajoran Prophet who incarnated herself in his human mother), he tells Kasidy that he does not know whether he will return in a year, or yesterday, or neither. We do not know in what form Sisko will reappear, and whether he is now, or will ever be, susceptible to death in the body.

In the end, Star Trek solves the perennial problem of death not by eliminating death, or by promising life after death, but by neutralizing fear of death. Consistent with Gene Roddenberry's dominating secular humanist perspective, it does so by arguing that death is natural, that it bestows meaning on existence, especially but not exclusively human existence, and that those who live a meaningful life need not concern themselves with the question of what happens when you die. In its narratives on transformation, Star Trek leaves open the possibility that other forms of existence await at least some of us. And the entire drama of Picard and Q closes the *Next Generation* series with the suggestion that all humanity might be evolving to some as yet unimagined existence. Whether such an existence might ultimately preclude or transform death seems hard to imagine, for over the ages death has given meaning to human life. It is death that affirms our existence.

Can Science Save
One's Soul?

WILLIAM CASSIDY

Roddenberry told me early on that his vision of the
24th century is that there's no hunger, no greed, and
that the point of life is to improve the quality of life.

—Patrick Stewart, quoted in
The Trekker's Guide to The Next Generation.

Most readers are accustomed to the notion that religions are
about salvation, that is, that the central goal of a religious life
is a better life to come in heaven. This is a central idea in
Christianity and Islam, but not so in Judaism, and not even a
goal in many forms of Buddhism and Hinduism. The goal of
salvation as the heavenly reward is not a universal concept. To
be sure, liberation from rebirth is a Hindu and Buddhist analog to Western concepts of salvation; the differences, however,

are striking. Buddhism, for instance, denies reality to any concept of a personal soul and, although it recognizes that heavens exist, they are not understood as the eternal abodes of the blessed. Rather, they are where the gods live and are as essentially impermanent as are all aspects of this life. Buddhist liberation is a far cry from Christian views of the heavenly reward.

Thus, the Christian notion is by no means universally paralleled in world religions, as charming and seductive as it might be to those of us consumed by the miseries of our present life. Christianity tends to conceive of salvation as something that is completed after death for all but perhaps a lucky few. Even those who believe that they are "saved" in this life by embracing Jesus look forward to the fulfillment of the heavenly reward. Although not a universal concept in religions, it has dominated Western culture for some time. It is not a concept that dominates Star Trek.

What Salvation?

Central to the outlook of Star Trek creator Gene Roddenberry was the rejection of institutionalized religion (e.g., Christianity) as superstition in favor of science and rationality, which could lead human beings into a new way of life. This passionate hope is woven into the imaginal future history of Earth between the twentieth century and the twenty-third century during the Original Series. A succession of devastating world wars and contact with the Vulcans lead the people of Earth to reorganize their society and join in the creation of the United Federation of Planets in 2161. By this time, religion seems to have become obsolete on Earth, along with internal war, racism, money, and a host of other ills. The view of Star Trek is that humans have evolved culturally and left the evils of previous ages in the past. Thus, the humanistic beliefs of Roddenberry, typical of much of the science-fiction literature of the 1950s and 1960s, were institutionalized in the Star Trek universe that he inaugurated.

Yet Star Trek also reflects the culture of the United States (and Canada to some extent). Religious concepts appear frequently in episodes, and religious issues that are part of contemporary American experience are frequently employed as themes and plots. Particularly in *Deep Space Nine* and *Voyager* there is tension between the humanistic foundation that Roddenberry built and religious themes that are presented in episodes produced in the later 1990s. Despite those more recent developments, we will argue that Roddenberry's humanism is the key to the central view of salvation in Star Trek.[1]

The notion of salvation from this-worldly danger is a key to understanding how the concept of salvation applies to Star Trek. In a this-worldly outlook, what could represent salvation? Certainly the "heavenly rewards" of some Star Trek religions are to be rejected as culture-specific beliefs with only limited, relative meaning and veracity. They don't seem much to apply to Starfleet personnel or to Federation folks in general. Religious answers to the question What is the meaning of life? have individual rather than universal application. Note that putting the issue in terms of the question of life's meaning refocuses it in a way that brings it more into line with the Star Trek reflections of Gene Roddenberry's humanism: There is no heavenly reward, so we must concentrate on this present universe. Here, too, there will be no perfection, so we must allow that improvement of the situation, rather than achieving a perfect world, is to be the goal.

For Star Trek, then, salvation is often presented in terms of finding the meaning of life. Salvation is found *in life*, not in mythological fantasies about perfection *after death*. Further, salvation is individualized; one person's meaning is not necessarily another's. Worf follows the Klingon code; Spock and Tuvok practice Vulcan logic. Each seeks to integrate himself into his chosen path. Likewise, Major Kira's faith in Bajoran religion provides her with a firm grounding from which she can weather the storms of *Deep Space Nine*. The model of salvation as the personal quest for the meaning of life is central to Star Trek.

Human Nature in
the Twenty-fourth Century

In "Encounter at Farpoint," the premiere episode of *Star Trek: The Next Generation*, Picard finds himself defending human beings in a fantastic court of law presided over by the extraordinary Q, who serves as both prosecutor and judge. Q's attire is suitably medieval, the charge being that humans are members of a backward and barbarous race, one so treacherous and violent that it deserves to be exterminated. As evidence, Q refers to episodes in the history of Earth showing "man's inhumanity to man." Picard does not dispute the facts but rather argues that the past is the past. Humanity has changed, Picard asserts; we have learned from our mistakes; we have improved.

This was precisely the hope of Gene Roddenberry, and he believed that science provided the key. His view is in line with the views of the Enlightenment and the spirit of modernism, with their myths of progress and theories of evolution. The terms *progress* and *evolution* are used freely in the dialogues between Q and Picard throughout *Next Generation*, indeed, throughout Star Trek. But the usage is also loose. Picard is not talking about the biological evolution of the human species when he makes claims for the moral superiority of humans in the Federation era. Humans are still the same species; he's talking about *cultural* progress. The reason we call attention to the distinction is that biological evolution is also an issue in Star Trek presentations about the destiny of human beings (more on that later).

By the twenty-third and twenty-fourth centuries, scientific and technological discoveries have nurtured cultural progress allowing human beings to become more moral. The Star Trek view seems to be in consonance with the ancient Chinese Confucian view that there is a reciprocal relationship between people and culture in terms of morality. Thus, a moral culture nurtures virtue in human beings, who then make the culture more moral. Education is the key to progress in this context. It is difficult, perhaps impossible, to maintain personal integrity in an immoral society, but the opposite is also true in a virtuous society. Classical Confucianism never voiced a unanimous opinion on the question of whether or not human nature was basically good. Confucius seems to have remained silent on the issue, and his philosophical descendants differed. Nevertheless, there was general agreement that humans may improve with hard work; we find Star Trek agreeing with this basic position.

We can contrast this view of human nature—that humans have the potential to be good or bad depending on the circumstances—with those of Christianity and Buddhism. The central Christian doctrine, dominated in this area by the idea of original sin, holds that humans are born in sin and may be saved only by the grace of God. Although there is controversy within Christianity regarding the extent to which humans can act to improve themselves in order to be saved by God, there is general agreement that the saving is done by God, not by human beings. We are incapable, because of our sinful nature, of saving ourselves.

Buddhism has a different view: Its most basic doctrine is that human beings can achieve awakening, or enlightenment. We must strive to do it ourselves. Although help is available through Buddha's teachings and, in some versions of Buddhism, through the aid of powerful "supernatural" beings, it is human effort that leads to liberation. Nevertheless, Buddhism has an unflinching view of life in this world. The First Noble Truth holds that life is not at all pleasant. It is ill, as opposed to well. We suffer a lot, and pleasure is brief and transitory. The Buddhist view of human life is a long way away from the optimism that Gene Roddenberry projected into the future.

Nevertheless, both Asian systems agree with Star Trek, and differ from Christianity, in emphasizing that progress toward the goal results from human effort. The natures of progress and the goal are, of course, different among these points of view, but they basically agree that human work is necessary. They also agree that education is the key that unlocks the door of progress. For Confucianism the education is in literature and morality; for Buddhism it is in philosophy and forms of mental discipline that we describe as meditation. For Star Trek, of course, the education is in science and technology. We don't wish to overemphasize the parallels we find here; the differences among these two spiritual philosophies and the fictional entertainment of the Star Trek universe are enormous.

At the end of "Encounter at Farpoint," Picard proves to Q that humans have changed. He doesn't simply argue the case;

he demonstrates it by freeing the trapped alien celestial jelly-fish so that it can go off with its mate. Rather than being grasp-ing, selfish, and violent, Picard shows that human beings have so enlarged their definition of humanity that the requirement for humane treatment of others extends beyond the human tribe—and beyond humanoid species—to alien species such as these enormous jellyfish space voyagers. Q relents for the moment, allowing that Picard has proved his point. Devoted fans know, of course, that the trial continues throughout the series and is central to the plot of the two-part finale, "All Good Things . . ." But there the test is not one of morality but of intelligence. The fact that humans have progressed is no longer contested. The question now is how far.

Salvation as the Personal Quest

One of the outstanding examples of this-worldly salvation ac-complished through a personal quest is found in the character of Odo, a *Deep Space Nine* ensemble character played by Rene Auberjonois. Odo is the constable, the chief of security of Deep Space Nine, the space station at the Wormhole near Ba-jor. He is one of the few officials who retain their posts when the station changes from Cardassian to Federation jurisdic-tion. Odo appears to be humanoid, but he is actually a shapeshifter, or Changeling. Initially his origins are unknown. He was found near Bajor in the Denorios Belt, the unstable re-gion of space in which the Wormhole is located. Taken to a bi-ological laboratory, Odo was raised by a Bajoran scientist and slowly developed his metamorphic abilities, but he always felt alienated from the culture of "solids." At first believed to be a unique life-form, Odo discovers the truth as the Deep Space

Nine personnel encounter aliens from the other side of the Wormhole—the Gamma Quadrant.

It turns out that Odo is a member of the race of shapeshifters called the Founders, who rule the Dominion as its gods, control that sector, and come to make war on the species on the Federation side of the Wormhole. Odo is thus in a difficult, nearly untenable situation, longing to join the fellow members of his species but remaining loyal to his comrades in the Federation. It is clear that his real identity, his real being, is with his kindred, who, on their own planet, dwell in the Great Link, a merged state, appearing as a calm, bronze-colored ocean.

Odo experiences the Great Link in an episode titled "Broken Link" (aired June 1996). In this story Odo becomes critically ill, and the only possibility of a cure lies in his return to his people. This is arranged by Commander Benjamin Sisko, who takes Odo into the Gamma Quadrant on Starship *Defiant*. They are met by a squadron commanded by the Female Shapeshifter, who informs Odo that they have caused his illness in order to return him to the Great Link so that he may be tried for the killing of another shapeshifter. The Great Link will cure him, but the charge is the most serious imaginable for a Founder. In all their history Odo is the first Changeling to kill another. The trial could end in a death sentence, but Odo has no choice, since the disease is mortal as well. Odo wades into the oceanic Great Link and disappears beneath its surface. Later he is cast out as a solid—a human being. The verdict is "guilty," and the punishment is to be cast out of the Great Link and to cease being a shapeshifter.

Once again, the biblical narrative of Genesis forms the subtext of a Star Trek plot. Odo's change of nature appears to be cast as a "fall from grace" or "expulsion from Eden." Odo falls from the "divinity" of the Founders to the mortality of the solids. Returning to the station, Odo takes up his job as chief security officer. When Sisko suggests that he take some time off, Odo declines. He prefers the routines of working. As he says:

> When I joined with the other Changelings in the Great Link I felt something I've never felt before. In that moment I knew I was home. For the first time I felt that I understood my people, their distrust of the solids, their willingness to do anything to protect themselves. And then, in an instant, it was all snatched away. I'm trapped inside this body. I can never rejoin the Great Link. My job is the only thing I have left.

Odo was granted a taste of paradise, but then it was withdrawn. Losing his Changeling status, he is no longer "one" with them, but he does retain the tantalizing memory of the Link. A loner, isolated by the essential difference of his very being as a shapeshifter, Odo has always felt estranged from the masses of humanoids around him. Now he is one *of* them—a humanoid—but for a moment he was one *with* his people, in a merging that goes beyond any communion that a humanoid could appreciate. There was individuality, but all were connected. (We wonder how the psychological connections of the Great Link might compare with the technological interconnectedness of the Borg.) For Odo, the Great Link represents salvation: It saves him from alienation and makes him whole, providing him with a meaning for his life. As Jewish and Christian traditions have sometimes imagined salvation as a quest to return to the paradisiacal state of the Garden in Genesis, so, too, Odo's quest is to return. For the rest of the series he will be torn between his strong loyalty to his Deep Space

Nine comrades and his kinship with the Founders, particularly after he once again becomes a shapeshifter. Having accomplished the first task in his quest—establishing his identity by finding his own people—he must now find a way to *atone* for his transgression so that he may once again become *at one* with them.

Many episodes develop Odo's conflict between his desire to be with his fellow Changelings and his faithfulness to Deep Space Nine and its agenda. By the end of the series Odo and Kira Nerys are lovers, and the Dominion is defeated. It is Odo who arranges the armistice by convincing the Female Shapeshifter, who commands the Dominion forces, to trust him. They link, and through this joining she is cured of the fatal disease that Federation agents created as a biological weapon against the Founders. Thus, Odo repays her in kind for saving him from the disease the Founders had given him. As this plague has infected the Changeling home world, they are all doomed without Odo's help. It is this salvation that Odo offers his people, and he is able to do it only because he is trusted both by the Federation and the Dominion. Curing the shapeshifter plague without a shapeshifter surrender would revive the war. But the Changelings do accept it and make peace with the Federation and its allies. Thus, they offer salvation to Odo as well, allowing him to return to their home world and join with them.

In the two-part final episode of *Deep Space Nine* ("What You Leave Behind," aired June 1999), Odo bids farewell to his beloved Kira on the island in the ocean of the Founders and returns to his people. He is fulfilled, apparently welcomed back into the Great Link. It is a powerful image of salvation, Star Trek–style. Odo embraces his destiny with his people, leaving behind his solid friends with regret, but without reluctance. He joins his fellow Changelings, wading into the copper ocean and then blending into it without a trace. The fact that the visual image reflects a traditional image of salvation in Hinduism should not be overlooked. Liberation, in some forms of Hinduism, is understood as the merging of the individual soul, or *atman*, with the universal soul, *Brahman*. In this Hindu merging all traces of individuality are lost, as the *atman* is not at all the personality of the individual, as is the case, for instance, with the Christian soul. In Hinduism, the personality is created by illusion and action, an aspect of the present life, not the soul. Thus, a root metaphor for this merging is that of a drop of water (the *atman*) with the ocean (*Brahman*). The drop becomes one with the ocean or, to express the situation more philosophically, the drop and the ocean are not two. In Odo's case, the individuality seems to be in some way retained, since his description of his previous Great Link experience suggests the retention of personal identity despite the sharing of form and mind.[2]

So Odo's heroic quest comes to a successful end. His quest for personal identity is fulfilled; he saves his people from destruction, and he returns to his long-lost home. This destiny is unique to Odo; it is incomprehensible for any humanoid solid to aspire to it. Although the basic model of salvation here is common to many Star Trek scenarios, the actual application of the model is utterly individualized. The android Data in *Next Generation*, for instance, provides an even more developed example in his quest to be more like humanoids, but space does not allow a full discussion of this popular character.

In Star Trek's general approach to salvation there is also a whiff of the so-called perennial philosophy associated with Houston Smith, among others, that (in the simplest terms) the various mystical paths lead to the top of the same mountain;

following *your* path is what's important. Thus, the truths of the doctrines of various religions are relative: All have symbolic truth, but none is uniquely, literally true. These perspectives no doubt underlie the intent of the writers and producers.

Star Trek Generations: Intensification of the Model

Star Trek: The Next Generation is set in the twenty-fourth century. The first episode, "Encounter at Farpoint," in which Jean-Luc Picard takes up command of the *Enterprise D,* is set in 2364, exactly 100 years after James T. Kirk begins his career as captain of the *Enterprise* in the Original Series. The film *Star Trek Generations* (1994) brings Kirk together with Picard as co-heroes, but the problem is that Kirk died in 2293 and the film is set in 2371. How are the two captains brought together? It's all part of the plot, which provides interesting material to discuss in the context of salvation.

Integral to the drama of the film *Generations* is a ribbonlike energy field that moves through space. It is called the Nexus, and it creates a localized temporal anomaly that traps beings who enter it. In the Nexus, one experiences bliss, a joy so intense that it is an end in itself. One can relive the best parts of one's life over and over, or live imagined lives in which all is pleasurable. The *Next Generation* character Guinan, played by Whoopi Goldberg, who lived in the Nexus for some time, describes it as "a place I've tried very, very hard to forget. . . . It was like being inside joy, as if joy was something tangible and you could wrap yourself up in it like a blanket; and never in my life have I ever been as content."

Guinan (among others) is forcibly removed from the Nexus during the accident that kills Kirk (whose body, by the way, was never recovered). She describes this trauma as being "pulled, ripped away. None of us wanted to go, and I would have done anything—*anything*—to get back there. Once I realized it wasn't possible, I learned to live with that." The conflict in the plot involves another former inhabitant of the Nexus, Soran (Malcolm McDowell), a scientist willing to do anything (such as destroying entire solar systems) to get back into the Nexus. Soran's family and his planet were destroyed by the Borg, but in the subjective reality of the Nexus he could live among them happily. In order to stop Soran, Picard considers entering the Nexus, but Guinan attempts to dissuade him with these words: "If you go, you're not gonna care about anything—not this ship, Soran, not me: nothing. All you'll want to do is stay in the Nexus. And you're not gonna want to come back."

The Nexus, with its life of individually programmed bliss, sounds a lot like heaven. Its delights could be spiritual, intellectual, sensual, depending on your own interests—perhaps all three. Although the Christian version of heaven doesn't usually appear to provide sensual delights, the Islamic heaven described in the Quran certainly does, as do the descriptions of the heavens of the Hindus and Buddhists. What Soran wants is one of the things most cherished by believers in heavenly salvation the world over: reunion with the cherished dead. He wants to live on with his wife and children. What's wrong with that?

Well, he is ruthless in achieving his goal. Thus, an analog to heaven is actually presented as an addiction. The Nexus brings pure bliss, like the rush of heroin. One will lie, steal, and even kill for that next fix; once there, you forget everything that is meaningful in life. Cosmic dope, not heaven, is the image for the Nexus. And Soran is fixing for another hit.

The addiction analogy ensures that the audience views Soran's quest as evil. His is a complex character, as we sympathize with his desire to return to his family. But that family is dead, the Nexus is a fantasy world, and he is despicably ruthless—a fine foil for the heroism of Picard and Kirk. An exchange between Soran and Picard on the theme of time (recall that the Nexus is a temporal anomaly; no time passes; existence there is eternal) is illustrative. Soran recalls that his devastating experience with the Borg showed him that, in life, time is the only constant.

> Soran: Time is like a predator, stalking you.
> Picard: It's our mortality that defines us, Soran. It's part of the truth of our existence.
> Soran: What if I told you I had found a new truth?
> Picard: The Nexus?
> Soran: Time has no meaning there. The predator has no teeth.

Picard has his own reasons to grieve, reasons that differ from but parallel Soran's. Picard never married and has no children. Family life means his brother, sister-in-law, and nephew, whom he loves dearly. But his brother and nephew have just been killed in a fire on Earth, so Picard, too, is bereft. His grief is as compelling as is Soran's. Mortality defines us, and part of that definition is grief at loss.

But that is the point. We are mortal. Life may be long, but it is finite. According to Star Trek, immortality just isn't in the cards for humans, as it would distort what we are. Mortality isn't just part of our condition, as Picard puts it, it is *essential* to our condition. Any attempt to mitigate that is fantasy, despite the promises of religions, despite the hopes of science. In Star Trek (as in life on Earth), humans are born to die; whatever meaning we find, we find here.

The latter part of the film bears out this view. During a suitably heroic struggle, Picard enters the Nexus. He first encounters an ideal personal situation. It is a Victorian-style Christmas Day and Picard is with his wife, children, and nephew. He is overcome by the joy of a life much wished for but never lived. His children are wonderful; the situation is perfect. But it's not right. Picard rejects this life and searches out James Kirk, who was never killed but had been pulled into the Nexus.

Kirk is living in a mountain cabin, identical to one he once owned, with a lover whom he plans to marry. He, too, wants the life he never lived. As he says to Picard, who has explained the situation of the Nexus,

> Kirk: You say history considers me dead. Who am I to argue with history?
> Picard: You're a Starfleet officer. You have a duty.
> Kirk: I don't need to be lectured by you. I was out saving the galaxy when your grandfather was in diapers. Besides which, I think the galaxy owes me one. . . . I was like you, so worried about duty and obligation that I couldn't see past my own uniform. And what did it get me? An empty house. Not this time. This time it's gonna be different.

Kirk chooses marriage over duty, but this is not the end of the conversation. The two go out horseback riding, and at one point Kirk urges his steed to jump a formidable gully. Afterward, he's disappointed. He changes his mind in this key speech:

I must have jumped that fifty times. Scared the hell out of me each time. Except this time, because it isn't real, nothing here is. Nothing here matters. You know, maybe it isn't about an empty house, maybe it's about that empty chair on the bridge of the *Enterprise*. Ever since I left Starfleet I haven't made a difference.

In the end, Kirk chooses reality over fantasy: Indeed, by the end of the film he chooses a meaningful death over a meaningless eternal life.

Due to the peculiar physical-temporal nature of the Nexus, Picard and Kirk are able to return to the location of Soran in the past, in time to defeat him and save if not the entire galaxy at least the nearby planetary system. But in the struggle Kirk is mortally wounded. The battle won, he says to Picard as he dies,

> Kirk: Did we do it? Did we make a difference?
> Picard: Oh yes, we made a difference. Thank you.
> Kirk: The least I could do for the captain of the *Enterprise*. It
>   was fun. Oh, my. . . .

And he dies, happily, preferring this death to life in the Nexus.

This is the dashing, boyish Kirk versus the cerebral, serious Picard, two very different captains agreeing on what is important in life: living well, duty, honor. Kirk would surely agree with Picard's final speech in the film, made on the shattered bridge of the *Enterprise D* to Riker:

> Someone once told me that time was a predator that stalked us all our lives, but I rather believe that time is a companion who goes with us on the journey and reminds us to cherish every

moment because they'll never come again. What we leave behind is not as important as how we've lived. After all, Number
One, we're only mortal.

Living the Good Life

What makes a good life? Judging by Star Trek, the first requirement is a satisfactory culture, represented by the United
Federation of Planets. Scientific and social development are
equally important. Good societies beget good people. A stable,
just, prosperous society is the first requirement. Need the society be interplanetary? Need it be large-scale?

Not according to Star Trek. Several episodes depict isolated
communities following idyllic lives in galactic Edens, lives that
are disrupted once visited by the *Enterprise* crew. The most
complex representative on this point are the Ba'ku on a planet
in the Briar Patch, a remote and dangerous part of the galaxy.
Their culture is presented in *Star Trek: Insurrection*, the latest
film in the series. They appear to live a pleasant, isolated life as
farmers, craftspeople, and artists; religious practices and beliefs are absent. They do have highly developed scientific
knowledge but intend to use it in limited ways necessary to
maintain their simple lifestyle. What's more, they do not age as
normal humanoids do due to the peculiar physics of the Briar
Patch. The Ba'ku also possess the ability to relativize time, to
slow the temporal sequence to the point where one can observe the wing beats of a hovering hummingbird. It is unclear
whether they alter perception or alter time (or whether it is
these distinctions that are faulty). Anij, their leader, is extremely attractive to, and attracted by, Picard.

Picard is charmed, and the plot demands that he resign from Starfleet, disobey direct orders from a commander, and engage in a violent action against Starfleet allies on behalf of the Ba'ku. The fact that Picard's cause is just—and that he will eventually succeed—goes without saying. As Picard parts from Anij in the final scene, we learn that the Federation will protect the Ba'ku so that they can live undisturbed; Picard plans to return, using some of the 300-odd vacation days he has accrued. As he says, "The 'mighty' Federation could learn a few things from this village." They kiss; he will be back.

The small village as paradise is a familiar scenario for urban cultures. Often, one finds strongly contrasting ideals between the life of action associated with cities and politics and the ideal of peaceful retirement of the countryside. The opposition is institutionalized in the Chinese tradition of Taoism, which posits an ideal of simple, isolated village life as the only truly fulfilling existence. As the classic Chinese text from several centuries before the time of Christ, the *Tao Te Ching*, puts it:

> Reduce the size and population of the state. Ensure that even though the people have tools of war for a troop or a battalion they will not use them; and also that they will be reluctant to move to distant places because they look on death as no light matter.
>
> Even when they have ships and carts, they will have no use for them; and even when they have armor and weapons, they will have no occasion to make a show of them.
>
> Bring it about that the people will return to the use of the knotted rope;
>> Will find relish in their food
>> And beauty in their clothes,
>> Will be content in their abode

And happy in the way they live.

Though the adjoining states are within sight of one another, and the sound of dogs barking and cocks crowing in one state can be heard in another, yet the people of one state will grow old and die without having any dealings with those of another. (Lao Tzu, *Tao Te Ching*, trans. D.C. Lau [Baltimore: Penguin, 1974], chap. LXXX, p. 142)

The Ba'ku echo this theme, albeit with the technology of the twenty-fourth century lurking just beneath. The Taoists tended to reject technology entirely, preferring the simplest ways to do things. In contrast, science and technology are integral to Star Trek.

The Inner Light

A model similar to that of a good life lived as its own reward is portrayed in the fifth-season *Next Generation* episode "The Inner Light." This episode won a Hugo Award in 1993 for the Best Dramatic Presentation and is one of the most compelling episodes in the entire series. Here, we will consider it in terms of the Star Trek model of salvation.

The crew of the *Enterprise* happens upon a strange probe of unknown design. It releases a beam of some sort that renders Picard unconscious. He's out for some twenty-five minutes, but during that time he lives half a life. Picard (now known as Kamin) finds himself on an uncharted planet, Kataan, inhabited by humans. Apparently he has been ill and is being cared for by a woman named Eline, who turns out to be his wife. Kamin is a craftsman, an iron weaver. Jean-Luc has problems coming to grips with the fact he is now someone else. It is as though Kamin has suffered from a combination of amnesia and a delusion about having another life as a Starfleet officer named Picard. He lives in the village of Ressik, is respected and well known there. The culture is simple; they have not developed space travel, although they do have scientists. The people of Kataan have developed aesthetic sensibilities; there is artwork in Kamin's home, typical of the community. The people of Ressik seem to be entirely free of religion.

As years pass, Picard becomes accustomed to his identity as Kamin. His initial efforts to contact the Federation were unsuccessful, and his preoccupation and restlessness disturb Eline. In one exchange she asks him, "Do you think your life is a dream?" He replies, "This is not my life!" Later, she tells him, "Never in any of the stories you have told me was there anyone who loved you as I do." This is a key; she *does* love him deeply. Slowly, he comes to accept his new life, becomes a better husband, a true member of the community. He also takes up music, learning to play the flute.

The episode skips back and forth between the *Enterprise* crew, working to bring the captain back to consciousness, and Kamin. Time passes on Kataan, with many years between some scenes. Kamin and Eline have children, who grow older. At one point Kamin remarks, "I always believed that I didn't need children to complete my life. Now I couldn't imagine life without them." His life is a happy one, but there are environmental problems on the planet. There is a drought that becomes worse during Kamin's lifetime. He fears that something dire is happening to the planet—and he is right. On the *Enterprise*, Geordi La Forge and Data determine that the probe originated on a planet (Kataan, of course), which was destroyed when its sun went supernova more than a thousand years before.

When Kamin's daughter Mirabor is of marriageable age, Picard urges her to wed soon. He, and she as well, fear that none of them will live out their lives before the planet is destroyed. "Seize the time," the father tells his daughter. "Live now. Make now always the most precious time. Now will never come again." She does marry and, as more time passes, bears Kamin's first grandchild. Eline dies, as does Kamin's good friend Batai.

In the final scene on Kataan, Kamin is an elderly man in his eighties. His daughter and granddaughter urge him to come outside, to see the "launch." He does so, donning his sun hat, for all must wear protection from the increasing solar radiation. When they are outside, he asks,

Kamin: What is it they're launching?

Mirabor: You know about it, Father. You've already seen it.

Kamin: Seen it? What are you talking about? I haven't seen any missile.

Batai: [Who has been dead for years, but nevertheless now appears to be in the prime of life.] Yes you have, old friend. Don't you remember?

Kamin: Batai!

Batai: You saw it just before you came here. We hoped our probe would encounter someone in the future. Someone who could be a teacher. Someone who could tell the others about us.

Kamin: Oh. Oh, it's me! Isn't it? I'm the someone. I'm the one it finds. That's what this launching is: a probe that finds me in the future.

Eline: [Also long dead; also appearing to be in the prime of life.] Yes, my love.

Kamin: Eline!

Eline: The rest of us have been gone a thousand years. If you remember what we were and how we lived, then we'll have
found life again.

Kamin: Eline. [The probe launches; all look to the sky.]

Eline: Now we live in you. Tell them of us, my darling.

Picard awakens on the deck of the bridge of the *Enterprise*.
Twenty-five minutes have passed, twenty-five minutes in
which he has lived a lifetime. Later, Riker enters the captain's
ready room with a small packet. "It was in the probe," he explains to Picard. The captain opens the package, and inside it
he finds his Ressikan flute. He takes it up and plays the tune
he so often played on Kataan, gazing out the window at the
countless stars of the galaxy.

Two aspects of this story present fundamental components
of Star Trek's humanistic perspective on salvation. The first is
the appeal of idyllic life in a small village. This theme balances
and complements the technologically complex but socially
simplistic life of heroic adventure that dominates the episodes.
Although James T. Kirk ultimately rejects a life of leisure for
duty, we can recall that the life he rejected on the Nexus is illu-
sory. And a life of family, love, and simple pleasures fits Picard's character perfectly. Duty to service and the lure of escape balance one another as two sides of the same golden
coin. Picard accepts his life as Kamin due to the love Eline has
for him. She represents the great hole in Captain Picard's life
(as for most Starfleet officers). Thus from the love 'em and
leave 'em relationships of the Original Series, Star Trek gradu-
ates to the depiction of romantic passion as a stable, loving,
mature relationship between man and woman. The two later
series, *Deep Space Nine* and *Voyager*, continue to portray romantic relationships in balanced, somewhat egalitarian terms.

The second fundamental component of Star Trek's humanistic perspective on salvation is that life is its own reward: We must make the most of it, living life to the full. The ingenious probe device that the Kataanians build is an attempt to preserve their lives and their culture. Note that the strategy, rather than presenting an encyclopedia of their culture, centers on only a few individuals. It tells a story that sketches the fundamental significance of their lives. Knowing that planetary annihilation is at hand, Eline tells Kamin, "If you remember what we were and how we lived, then we'll have found life again." That is their salvation; that is their monument. Although Ferengi, Bajoran, and other "local" religions in the Star Trek universe posit heavenly reward salvation scenarios comparable to those of contemporary Western religions, these are minor themes. The central Star Trek concept is humanistic and secular: A good life lived is its own reward. Thus, Kamin tells Mirabor, "Seize the time. Live now." Death is inescapable, but life can be meaningful. Whatever else can be said, Star Trek's characters find meaning in living out their lives.

The Chase

We conclude by exploring how Star Trek manipulates scientific ideas to make the case that evolution itself contains aspects that might be experienced as numinous or sacred. This notion is depicted in the sixth-season *Next Generation* episode "The Chase" (aired April 1993).

How can a secular scientific notion such as evolution be understood as sacred? Let us be clear on this issue: Our argument is that, regardless of the many pitfalls of using religious terminology in this context, we can discern a spiritual dimension in Star Trek's depiction of scientific theories. In Star Trek it is scientists who refine human understanding of the laws of nature, the laws that rule the universe. True, those laws can be manipulated, for instance, by the Q Continuum and other powerful beings. And because the humanistic view central to Star Trek rejects any supernatural reality beyond physical reality, we must dig deeper to make our point.

In "The Chase," Captain Picard is visited on the *Enterprise* by his former archaeology professor, Doctor Richard Galen. The professor brings his former star student a gift, an ancient artifact called a Kurlian *naiskos*. It looks like a ceramic bust of some Kurlian, and it opens to reveal several figurines inside. Picard identifies the artifact correctly, even to the identity of its creator, the third-dynasty Master of Tarquin Hall. The *naiskos* is some 12,000 years old, a rare specimen indeed. The respect that Picard displays for his old professor is salutary, but his reverence for the *naiskos* is more marked. Its antiquity and rarity make it all the more valuable, and Picard treats it as holy.[3]

The complicated plot centers on Galen's discovery that DNA samples from nineteen different worlds spread across the galaxy have similar protein configurations despite their sources in different species from different planets. Why? How can this be? Apparently Galen was on the track of these answers in his travels to obscure planets. But he is murdered during his journey, and the *Enterprise* arrives too late to save him. It is this mystery that Picard determines to solve.

It turns out that Klingons and Cardassians are on Galen's trail. They have fragments of DNA that are part of the sequence, but which Galen had not yet collected. With the grudging assistance of these aliens, *Enterprise* scientists are able to determine that the DNA collection is a complex artifact itself. It is at once a composite genetic code derived from life-forms indigenous to various planets, a galactic map that indicates the locations of solar systems billions of years ago, and (astonishingly) a computer program. As Picard describes it, "It's four billion years old, a computer program from a highly advanced civilization, and it's hidden in the very fabric of life itself. Whatever this program contains could be the most profound discovery of our time, or the most dangerous. And the professor knew that."

While Picard leans toward the scientific discovery side of the equation, the Klingons and Cardassians have other views, which perhaps reflect their own cultural biases. For the Klingons, the program should create a weapon of incredible power; the Cardassians see it as a key to an unlimited energy source. Yet no one is sure, and the only way to find out is to visit the final planet revealed in the code's map, Ur; all three parties convene there. The mood is edgy enough, but when they are joined by a Romulan delegation that has been following their progress in a cloaked ship, the situation deteriorates. Klingons are rather fractious allies of the Federation, and Cardassians had been at war with the Federation until a recent armistice. The Romulan Star Empire is the enemy of all of three civilizations; none trusts the other. Weapons are drawn, and threats are made.

Picard and Doctor Crusher clandestinely take a genetic sample of an indigenous plant and analyze it in their tricorder. Suddenly the tricorder is reprogrammed by the sample, the last bit of the code, to emit a holographic image. This sudden epiphany presents a female humanoid who explains the mystery that has led them to this planet:

> You're wondering who we are; why we have done this. How has it come that I stand before you, the image of a being from so long ago?

Life evolved in my planet before all others in this part of the galaxy. We left our world, explored the stars, and found none like ourselves. Our civilization thrived for ages, but what is the life of one race compared to the vast stretches of cosmic time? We knew that one day we would be gone, that nothing of us would survive. So we left you.

Our scientists seeded the primordial oceans of many worlds where life was in its infancy. The seed codes directed your evolution toward a physical form resembling ours: this body you see before you, which is, of course, shaped as yours is shaped. For you are the end result.

The seed codes also contained this message which was scattered in fragments on many different worlds. It was our hope that you would have to come together in fellowship and companionship to hear this message, and, if you can see and hear me, our hope has been fulfilled.

You are a monument, not to our greatness, but to our existence. That was our wish—that you, too, would know life and would keep alive our memory. There is something of us in each of you, and so, something of you in each other. Remember us.

During this speech the various humanoids change their attitudes, from belligerence to rapt attention upon the Ur-humanoid. Phasers drop to their sides as they focus on the messenger. It's an extraordinary moment, but it doesn't last. As soon as the message is over, the hologram disappears. The Klingons and the Cardassians are infuriated that there is "nothing of value" to be gained for all their effort and depart the planet immediately. The *Enterprise* lingers for a few days, accomplishing some necessary maintenance and repair on the vessel. Picard receives a message from the Romulan commander just before they leave the area:

Romulan: It would seem that we are not completely dissimilar,
after all, in our hopes or in our fears.
Picard: Yes.
Romulan: Well, then, perhaps one day . . .
Picard: One day.

The fact that a Romulan grasps the larger picture is remarkable, as the Romulan race is the most antagonistic. That message in and of itself carries power, just as the visual scene creates awe. The female messenger is played by Salome Jens, the same actress who portrays the Female Shapeshifter in *Deep Space Nine*. Her facial makeup is intended to suggest a prototypical humanoid, with heavy features, smooth skin, devoid of hair, clearly female. We could call her Eve, but the story has no resonance with the biblical creation myth. The fact that she represents the Great Mother, the mother of all life, is another possible parallel from numerous Terran mythological traditions. In fact, Star Trek is portraying something a little different: Creation is managed by biological species, not a god or goddess, whether transcendent or immanent.

This "scientific" story of creation intends to shape the cultures of Star Trek humanoids. The original intent is salvific, in the humanistic terms that Star Trek supports. All humanoid species are really one, like all disparate cultures in the galaxy. In becoming one they heal the terrors of war, poverty, and intolerance (at least if they follow the Federation model). Not all Star Trek civilizations do so, however, as is symbolized by the Klingon and Cardassian dismissal of the message from the creators. But the Romulan, unexpectedly, gets it, going so far as to engage in tentative communication with his enemy Picard. From such small beginnings great events may grow.

The image of the Kurlian *naiskos* becomes potent. It represents the individual as a single entity, but as the depiction of a community of individuals as well it symbolizes a central concept of personhood and community within the Star Trek universe. It represents the microcosm of the individual and, in terms of Star Trek, the macrocosms of community and genus. Just as a healthy individual has negotiated a harmony among "the many voices inside the one," so, too, a culture that embraces differences within itself (ethnicities, political divisions, etc.) without prejudice, allowing multiplicity within unity, moves beyond limited self-interest toward promoting the welfare of both the whole and its parts. This secular cultural "evolution" also may have spiritual aspects. Yet it is an ideal that represents personal as well as cultural salvation. The hope of the original humanoid civilization was to create a greater, more diverse community by "seeding" the galaxy with the potential for the eventual evolution of kindred humanoid species. Their dream was that this diverse community, through the mystery of the code, could come to realize its original unity again.

Thus, this concept of evolution blends science and religion. Evolution (in the genetic sense of the origin of humanoid species) is portrayed as being by design. The fact that the design is created by humanoids, rather than by any god, is an essential point. Human beings from Earth are simply one of the species, one with the Klingons and Romulans. In the words of the Ur-humanoid, "There is something of us in each of you, and so, something of you in each other." "The Chase" was a scientific and personal quest, leading to new knowledge of an unparalleled order in the universe. Likewise, the quest for order in civilized existence has, in the humanistic milieu of Star Trek, acquired religious significance.

The final exchange between Picard and Q at the end of "All Good Things. . . " (the final episode of *Next Generation*) seems relevant:

> Q: You just don't get it, do you, Jean-Luc. The trial never ends. We wanted to see if you had the ability to expand your mind and your horizons. And for one brief moment, you did.
>
> Picard: When I realized the paradox.
>
> Q: Exactly. For that one fraction of a second you were open to options you had never considered. *That* is the exploration that awaits you: not mapping stars and studying nebulae, but charting the unknown possibilities of existence.

The unknown possibilities of existence represent mystery in the Star Trek universe, just as improving the quality of life is the point of existence. There is no God to condemn us for being sinful; life in this world is not a painful trap from which we must escape. Star Trek charges the universe with optimism: We hold our salvation in our own hands.

Epilogue: Saving "The World as We Know It"

"In my century we don't succumb to revenge. We have a more evolved sensibility."
"Bullshit."

—An exchange between Jean Luc Picard and Lily Sloane in *Star Trek: First Contact*

For more than three decades Star Trek has put forth the premise that Terran culture was transformed by two events: a major cataclysm, and a salvific encounter. Although we are given sketchy information about these, crucial details are provided in the film *Star Trek: First Contact*. In a time line–twisting tale, the crew of the *Enterprise* (the cast from *Next Generation*) must follow a Borg sphere (which emerges from a Borg cube) through a chronological tunnel into the past. The Borg intend to disrupt human history in the past so that they can assimilate Earth and preclude a future Borg defeat at the hands of the United Federation of Planets. Picard must repair damage the Borg have already caused so that human history can unfold the way it should have.

The Borg have chosen a particular moment to invade Earth: April 4, 2063. In North America ten years have passed since the Third World War. As Commander William Riker notes, "Most of the major cities have been destroyed, very few cities left, six hundred million dead." This is the scenario conjured up by Q when he places Picard on trial for the crimes of humanity in "Encounter at Farpoint" and "All Good Things . . . ": All that remains of justice is a rag-tag group of survivors, rife with anger, who pass judgment on offenders with little or no structure of law. The scruffy survivors of *First Contact* appear to be a desperate cell of frightened humanity, hanging on in a settlement located by an abandoned missile complex in central Montana. They wear nondescript clothing and retain a few archaic remnants of North American civilization. This is a familiar scenario famous in science fiction: as broken-down and warring factions vie for power, a profound hopelessness pervades humanity. Possible leaders emerge, with different agendas. The savior in *First Contact* has a single, unheroic desire: to use his technological expertise to earn enough money to find oblivion in some tropical paradise. The vulnerability of mankind makes it an easy target—whether for assimilation or rescue. The *Enterprise* crew knows this moment well.

Star Trek's history of the future records that at precisely this moment a somewhat lunatic but endearing drunk named Zefram Cochrane has discovered the secret of warp drive—the ability to travel faster than light. Having converted a missile into a primitive spaceship, he will test it on April 5, 2063. As he does so he will attract the attention of a passing ship belonging to, of all beings in the universe, the Vulcans. As counselor Deanna Troi explains to a recalcitrant Cochrane, they will be "on a survey mission . . . they have no interest in Earth: too primitive." Riker continues: "When they detect a warp signature from your ship . . . they decide to alter their course and make first contact with Earth right here. . . . It is one of the pivotal moments in human history, Doctor. You get to make first contact with an alien culture right here, and after you do, everything begins to change." And, finally, from Troi: "It unites humanity in a way that no one ever thought possible when they realize they are not alone in the universe. Poverty, disease, war . . . they'll all be gone within the next fifty years." It is this transformation from defeat and disintegration to enlightened triumph that the *Enterprise* hopes to rescue and the Borg hope to destroy. The Federation, Starfleet Academy, indeed everything in *Star Trek* tries to portray the future as an idyll of human potential. As Picard describes it: "The acquisition of wealth is no longer the driving force in our lives. We work to better ourselves and the rest of humanity." And as Kirk observes in *Star Trek IV: The Voyage Home*, money as such does not exist in the future (although fans will know that "gold-pressed latinum" does a pretty good imitation).

Those familiar with the concepts of eschatology and apocalypse will find all of this remarkably familiar. Many religious traditions have proposed an endtime, a moment of complete or near-total destruction. It is from such a disaster that a new, perfected world will emerge, much like the Phoenix, a symbol of life rising from the ashes and the name of Zefram Cochrane's warp ship. Indeed, by some accounts, from Hinduism to Judaism and Christianity, the endtime scenario *may only come to pass* when the evil, destructive forces of the world have triumphed, chaos and disintegration have ensued, and a cataclysm of fire has cleared the way for the Golden Age, the Perfected World, the New Jerusalem, or the Satya or Krita Yuga. Of course, from the perspective of South Asian traditions, such events occur in a circular pattern, over and over eternally; the more linear Western theologies understand this as a "once and final" occurrence. But descriptions of the new existence almost always use Troi's image of freedom from poverty, disease, and war. Lily Sloane, Cochrane's assistant, envies the world to which Picard returns, as well she should. The fact that salvation for the deserving comes "from above" rings true here, except that the image of the ministering angel is a Vulcan with pointy ears, a parody of human demonic imagery. This is a secular humanistic apocalypse, after all, despite Cochrane's invocation—"sweet Jesus!"—as his converted missile achieves light speed.

Throughout this volume we have referred to Gene Roddenberry's vision of the future as being a much better place than ours. Roddenberry's hope, portrayed and developed in Star Trek over the years, is that Terran culture will be transformed by conflict and scientific progress but that crucial changes will come via contact with alien races in interstellar space travel. Star Trek is about this human transformation from a deeply flawed cultural situation to one that is, although never perfected, capable of vast improvement. Essential to this improvement is, of course, interaction with alien species resulting in an ever-widening understanding of "humanity" to include humanoid and even nonhumanoid beings such as the android Data. As we have argued, in consonance with the basic concepts of science, this process is ongoing. Just as scientific knowledge constantly expands, so, too, cultural transformation is an ongoing phenomenon: New problems arise, new information appears, new solutions are developed. The foundation for this transformation is twofold: physical science wedded to a humanistic culture of tolerance.

Although Star Trek places the evolution of human and Federation society in a secular, scientific frame of reference, we find it worthwhile to point out that human cultures have tended to understand this transformation through religious lenses. To be sure, many historical religions have been deeply conservative elements of their cultures. But religions have also become agents of cultural change and transformation.

Religious transformation tends to work on the personal and social levels simultaneously. That is, the obligation found in most contemporary religions—to improve oneself through moral formation or asceticism—is often linked to a social obligation of improving the world. In Confucianism self-culti-vation develops superior individuals, who then lead society toward a more moral way of life. Traditional religions that view human life as being problematic usually claim that the problem is built in; Christianity does so with the doctrine of original sin. Human transformation is often linked to the at-tempt to turn away from sin and toward God: Aspects of this motif are often present in forms of Judaism, Christianity, and Islam. The faithful are taught to follow divinely revealed law in order to improve themselves and the world as a whole.

In Asia, both Sanatana Dharma (Hinduism) and Buddhism claim that human transformation can be accomplished through disciplined attempts to overcome ego and achieve a higher perspective. Both use karma theory and the illusion of *maya* to explain human weakness and failure and offer the goal of enlightenment as the ultimate resolution to worldly suffering. The myriad yogas ("disciplines" or "teachings"), in-cluding the meditation systems popularized in the West, seek this goal of liberation, or awakening toward an altered point of view that allows one to see reality as it is. It is commonly as-sumed in most forms of Buddhism and Hinduism that these paths of transformation will also make the practitioner a more moral agent. Although the impulse toward social transformation is not presented the same way in these Asian traditions as it has been in the modern West, it is a misrepresentation to claim that social benefits are entirely absent. In the many forms of Hinduism, to understand and fulfill holy Dharma (duty, responsibility, identity, one's role and place) is not only to improve one's own karma (as manifested in future incarnations) but to better the larger world.

Religions often emphasize, therefore, the necessity and the utility of transformation, both for the individual and the group, toward an ideal state of existence and a new understanding of reality. They do so in the conviction that these goals are in agreement with divine or eternal will, however it is characterized. In other words, religion seeks its goals based upon special knowledge, information, experience, and wisdom. In this it is not so different from science and shares much in common with humanism. The question really is this: What is the source of the knowledge, information, experience, and wisdom from which the teachings are derived, and whence does it derive its authority? This is where the battleground is often located in modern discourse.

How does this fit in the context of Star Trek? The lasting and growing popularity of Star Trek suggests that the distinction between scientific/humanistic transformation and religious/spiritual transformation is breaking down. That is, the writers and producers of Star Trek, in their creative treatment of religious themes in *Next Generation*, *Deep Space Nine*, *Voyager*, and the most recent movies, are using scientific and humanistic frames to discuss transformations that have traditionally been understood through the lens of spiritual and religious concepts.

In Star Trek, the quest for scientific knowledge does not necessarily preclude the religious quest for knowledge of ultimate reality. In fact, they may sometimes be seen to exist in consonance. At first blush this would seem to stand opposite Roddenberry's vision. Didn't he reject religion and forbid it to have a part in Starfleet? Well, yes, but no single religion is proposed as a model, neither a contemporary Terran faith nor one of the fictional alien religions. It is more of a religious sensibility that is found in Star Trek, perhaps akin to some form of spirituality as it is understood in modern Western cultures. There is nothing denominational or exclusive about this sensibility.

Rather than being connected to a particular religion, this theme centers on knowledge, especially knowledge of reality. Consider for the moment that the scientific method requires changing one's mind from time to time, as data and theory-building require. At times this happens on a large scale, as with the shift from the Newtonian worldview to Einstein's relativity theory and quantum physics. Such fundamental transformations, or paradigm shifts, change the nature of reality. Our conception and thus perception of reality change dramatically. These changes enlarge our view and bring us closer to knowledge of reality.

Likewise, descriptions of mystical experiences and their human impacts portray a fundamental transformation of conception and perception. The physical world is still there, and it looks the same to everyone else, but to the mystic it has all transformed. Now it appears as it really is; now the mystic has knowledge of reality. We're not claiming that the yogin and the scientist have identical views of reality. Put simply, Star Trek seems to bring these two forms of transformation into convergence. Thus, as characters move rapidly through time and space and realities alter, the character of their experience becomes religious or spiritual rather than scientific or secular. At the extreme edge, distinctions between spiritual and scientific have as much relevance as those between wave and particle. Perhaps the most obvious image of this occurs when Spock, in *Star Trek VI: The Undiscovered Country*, appears in his quarters: He represents the incarnation of rationality in a monk's robe, deep in meditation, seeking understanding, as the Star Trek world he knows undergoes its own transformation.

Can a TV series, designed for entertainment purposes and directed primarily toward the North American audience, serve as an adequate or approximate measure, or mirror, of the transformations of culture over time? Our studies of this phenomenon suggest that it can. More than that, it can describe ways in which culture copes with transformations, in both constructive and destructive ways.

The "scientistic" approach has been defined not as faith in science itself but as a willingness to place final authority in the human ability to resolve, through science, the questions that have challenged and tormented our species (see the last chapter in Morton Klass, *Ordered Universes: Approaches to the Anthropology of Religion*, Boulder, Colo: Westview Press, 1995). Gods may or may not exist, but in the end humankind has the ability to answer many questions by way of scientific enterprise. This is where Star Trek began in the 1960s, where Gene Roddenberry was most comfortable. The fundamentalist way (see Klass, cited above) has less to do with current political-religious fundamentalisms than with the attitude many people have developed in response to the perceived challenge of science. Here, the final authority on ultimate matters rests with divinity. Science can provide reliable and useful information, and technology need not be rejected or disdained; but "revealed" knowledge contained in sacred texts and traditions provides the answers. It is possible to see the *Deep Space Nine* series as following this approach. The Prophets *are* the ultimate authority in that series and have influenced events over vast stretches of time in order to achieve a goal that is dimly perceived by humanoids. The postrationalist way (again, see Klass) is characterized by a collective rejection of the assumption that there is a single, certain source of knowledge. Adherents to this ideology reject exclusivist claims to truth by either science *or* religions, as well as any dogma that limits the options. There is a lively skepticism toward the fundamentalist ideologies as well as a suspicion of the scientistic approach, an openness toward beliefs and discoveries worldwide, and an attitude of acceptance of one another. Crucial to postrationalists is that the quest must continue. Klass defines that quest as the search for "meaning and comfort in a world where literally anything is possibly true and nothing can be known for certain" (p. 162). Star Trek has mirrored the tension between the scientific and religious worldviews since its first episode.

Today there is a perceptible and developing tension between the scientific and religious worldviews. The series has encouraged several generations to imagine the implications of the sciences of the stars; it has raised awareness of the issues, the meanings, and the possibilities of such discovery; it has participated in a transformation of awareness that has characterized our space and time. Is it not possible to see some form of religious sensibility at work as well? The issues that entertain us on the screen—the origins of the universe and our lives within it, its purpose, its design, its end, its meaning—are the concern of the sciences and religion. Through Star Trek we are catapulted to a place where science and religion may, perhaps fruitfully, coexist. Religion has not retreated in the face of modern science, as many once believed it would. And religion need not see itself as opposed to modern science. Whatever its sources of authority, structure, and knowledge, religion must draw upon the power of the human imagination to survive. If it cannot be imagined, it cannot be believed. In the scientific world, it is imagination that fuels discovery and the transformation of knowledge.

There are dangers in this intersection of concerns, of course, not the least of which is apparent in the exchange between Picard and Lily Sloane quoted at the beginning of this chapter. For all of Picard's "evolved sensibility," some things never change in the Star Trek future, and one of these is the human capacity for arrogance. Whether it occurs in Starfleet captains, among the scientific community, or among religious circles, it is a quality likely to lead people astray. Yet Picard acknowledges Lily's insight and honesty, stating how he will miss her. It is in the transformation of awareness and the transmutation of arrogance to humility that religion has achieved some of its most transcendent moments. The representations of religion in Star Trek, although hardly providing transcendent experience, seem to suggest this possibility in its finest moments.

We have explored the range and limitations of Star Trek's religious imagination and its theological speculation in this volume. If "the world as we know it" is salvageable, these are the moments that suggest a path to that goal.

List of Series,
Episodes, and Films

List of Series and Episodes Cited in the Text (with Original Airdates)

Star Trek (Original Series)

"The Alternative Factor"   March 30, 1967
"Amok Time"   September 15, 1967
"The Apple"   October 13, 1967
"Bread and Circuses"   March 15, 1968
"The Empath"   December 6, 1968
"The Enemy Within"   October 6, 1966
"Mirror, Mirror"   October 6, 1967
"Space Seed"   February 16, 1967
"Where No Man Has Gone Before"   September 22, 1966
"Who Mourns for Adonais?"   September 22, 1967
"Wolf in the Fold"   December 22, 1967

Star Trek: The Next Generation

"All Good Things . . . "   May 23, 1994
"The Best of Both Worlds, Parts I and II"   June 18, 1990 and
    September 24, 1990
"The Chase"   April 26, 1993
"Darmok"   September 30, 1991
"Datalore"   January 18, 1988
"Deja Q"   February 5, 1990
"Descent, Parts I and II"   June 21, 1993 and September 20,
    1993
"Devil's Due"   February 4, 1991
"Elementary, Dear Data"   December 5, 1988
"The Emissary"   June 29, 1989
"Encounter at Farpoint"   September 28, 1987
"Heart of Glory"   March 21, 1988
"Hide and Q"   November 23, 1987
"I, Borg"   May 11, 1992
"Inheritance"   November 22, 1993
"The Inner Light"   June 1, 1992
"Journey's End"   March 28, 1994
"Justice"   November 9, 1987
"Lessons"   April 5, 1993
"Man of the People"   October 5, 1992
"Masks"   February 21, 1994
"The Next Phase"   May 18, 1992
"Phantasms"   October 25, 1993
"Remember Me"   October 22, 1990
"Rightful Heir"   May 17, 1993
"Ship in a Bottle"   February 1, 1993
"Skin of Evil"   April 25, 1988
"Sub Rosa"   January 31, 1994

"Time's Arrow, Parts I and II"   June 15, 1992 and September
   21, 1992
"Tin Man"   April 23, 1990
"Transfigurations"   June 4, 1990
"Where No One Has Gone Before"   October 26, 1987
"Where Silence Has Lease"   November 28, 1988
"Who Watches the Watchers?"   October 16, 1989
"Yesterday's Enterprise"   February 19, 1990

Star Trek: Deep Space Nine

"The Assignment"   October 28, 1996
"Battle Lines"   April 25, 1993
"Body Parts"   June 10, 1996
"Broken Link"   June 17, 1996
"Children of Time"   May 5, 1997
"Emissary"   January 3, 1993
"The Emperor's New Cloak"   February 3, 1999
"Favor the Bold"   October 27, 1997
"Homefront"   January 1, 1996
"The Reckoning"   April 29, 1998
"Shadows and Symbols"   October 7, 1998
"Tears of the Prophets"   June 17, 1998
"What You Leave Behind, Parts I and II"   June 2, 1999

Star Trek: Voyager

"Caretaker, Parts I and II"   January 16, 1995
"Coda"   January 29, 1997
"Barge of the Dead"   October 6, 1999

"Emanations"   March 13, 1995
"The Q and the Gray"   November 27, 1996
"Scorpion"   September 3, 1997
"Unity"   February 12, 1997

Star Trek Feature Films (with Original Release Dates)

Star Trek The Motion Picture   December 7, 1979
Star Trek II: The Wrath of Khan   June 4, 1982
Star Trek III: The Search for Spock   June 1, 1984
Star Trek IV: The Voyage Home   November 26, 1986
Star Trek V: The Final Frontier   June 9, 1989
Star Trek VI: The Undiscovered Country   December 6, 1991
Star Trek Generations   November 18, 1994
Star Trek: First Contact   November 22, 1996
Star Trek: Insurrection   December 11, 1998

NOTES

Introduction

1. When we say we have chosen to treat Star Trek as a coherent text, we analyze the episodes and films as we encounter them, as most viewers have encountered them, without engaging in much attempt to determine the intentions of the episodes' writers. We infer, therefore, the authors' intentions from the texts themselves. The same thing is true for sacred scriptures throughout history, including many works central to the study of religion. We are accustomed to interpreting texts and artifacts without recourse to authorial intent. And even though our focus is the texts of Star Trek, it would be irresponsible to ignore Roddenberry's expressed views on religion and related subjects, especially given the control that Roddenberry exerted over Star Trek. Although raised in a Baptist family, Roddenberry came early to the conclusion that religion made no sense. For him, religion was full of misstatements and reaches of logic that he couldn't agree with. Instead, he came to concur with the humanist position that human beings have free will and can with critical thinking solve problems without outside or supernatural help. This view characterizes the dominant perspective in Star Trek.

Chapter 2

1. This concept is sometimes difficult for Westerners to appreciate, as it parallels our default ethical dualism and contrasts it decisively. In Taoism good and evil are relativized. They are products of human judgment,

not part of the cosmic fabric. Indeed, the *Tao Te Ching* explains quite pointedly that the cosmos is not concerned with human understandings of good and evil. Interpretations of good and evil are provisional human decisions, which can be overturned because of new data or deepened understanding. They are relative.

2. We don't have the space to tell all the story chronologically. What we learn is that there *is* a cosmic opposition of good and evil in the Bajoran religion, that it is central to the mission of the Emissary, Benjamin Sisko, and that this religious tale is at the heart of what *Deep Space Nine* has really been all about. The humanist and secular vision of Star Trek becomes, by the end of *Deep Space Nine*, primarily religious—and based in the dualistic myths and symbols of Christianity!

3. Benjamin Sisko, as we have already explained, was born not of an ordinary woman but of the Sarah Prophet, who came to Earth and became incarnate in a woman in order to bear this son of a human father, then returned to the Celestial Temple. This is revealed in "Shadows and Symbols," an episode that is part of the final sequence.

4. Even though the Prophets and Pah-wraiths exist within the realm of science, they nevertheless function more like supernatural beings. The presentation is ambiguous, and this ambiguity seems to be intended. The Prophets answer Sisko's prayer; he is a human being from Earth as well as a Starfleet officer. We are thus no longer in the realm of localized, alien religions.

Chapter 3

1. The Kai herself is a religious specialist of considerable interest. In Bajoran culture it is the Kai who serves to translate visions given by the orbs to the people.

2. The fact that Bajor was brutally occupied by the cruel Cardassians for many generations helps to explain why its people are so religious, although the truth is much more complex. The fact that pain, suffering, and death push people toward religion is one of the fundamental truths of religious phenomena. However, from the first episode to the last, *Deep Space Nine* seems willing to entertain the notion that some religious beliefs may be based on actual experience in a reality we can recognize, and may work in constructive (albeit mysterious) ways to achieve worthy goals. Such beliefs are always fraught with danger, of course.

3. In the Nexus one's own conception of paradise is projected into reality: Whatever one desires most is created. Time becomes malleable

and inconsequential, events may occur in any order, determined only by one's will. Whatever has been lost may be found and experienced again and again as desired. Whatever haunts and troubles the soul may be addressed and resolved. If we were to reimagine the biblical Paradise according to our fondest hopes, it might well be the Nexus.

4. Astrophysics, the scientific discipline devoted to the study of the same phenomena, also constructs meaning by observation and the interpretation of relationships. It provides alternate scenarios to the traditional religious ones and is preferable to the scientifically minded (whether religious or not) because of its basis in logic and reason. To be sure, the scientific study of the skies has altered our understanding of them considerably and revealed fascinating possibilities apart from what religion has been able to provide. Interestingly, the Big Bang theory, the expanding nature of the universe, as well as the certainty that our sun will eventually self-destruct and the universe might even reverse its outward flow and contract—all provide parallels to cosmological and apocalyptic images generated by religious traditions throughout history.

Chapter 4

1. It is Kirk, the classic Western hero, who takes matters into his own hands. The perspective of Spock is a subtext, the other side of Kirk's heroic persona, the yin and yang; both fail individually, but together they triumph. This pattern repeats itself throughout their association and, in part, explains their friendship over so many years.

2. Such ceremonies are designed to assist the individual and community in the formal acknowledgement of life's transitions. Equally important is the fact that such transitions are traditionally understood as dangerous. The individual and group are vulnerable during times of radical change, although the precise understanding of the nature of this danger varies from culture to culture, tradition to tradition. The end result can include a fundamental shift in philosophy or theology. On the personal level, physical change and perhaps a change of name often accompany the more subtle psychological factors. The term often used to describe this period of vulnerability is "liminality," the state of being neither this nor that, neither here nor there. Any American teenager in our culture is aware of the dangerous nature of this transitional time.

3. Individual and cultural identity are forged largely by the stories we tell ourselves and each other over time; storytelling is a creative act for the creator as much as for the audience. A really good story touches on

immortality and, as is true of Gilgamesh, steps out of its original time and space. The Ramayana, one of the most popular ancient stories of South Asia and a tale of heroism in the context of the traditional values and sensibility of India, lives on in both India and much of Asia with renewed vigor in the contemporary era, taking on political implications of considerable power. To be actively engaged in the mythology of a culture is to participate in a sense of eternity.

4. This is also a story about the perceived duality of life and death. In the context of "The Inner Light" Picard's life on the *Enterprise* ends while he lives a long, full life on Kataan as Kamin. That life, however, must end, which leads to a return to life on the *Enterprise*. In other words, Picard dies, lives, dies, and is reborn. Similarly, the residents of Kataan, dead for a millennium, come back to life—and then die again in Picard. Understanding life and death not as opposites, or mutually exclusive realities, but as part of a continuum understood as circular would transform one's approach to himself and the world. It could be argued that this is precisely what happens to Picard. It is certainly what happens to the sages of South Asian mythology.

5. The flute reappears in later episodes, always when Picard is pensive or meditative, and once when he dares to love again ("Lessons"). And the fact that his life on Kataan lasted a mere twenty-five minutes is a mystery easily compared to South Asian mythologies such as the stories of Narada and Markandaya.

Chapter 5

1. The original title of the screenplay (*In Thy Image*) and the generative embrace of Kambatta and Collins both derive from the creation narrative of Genesis 1:26: "Then God said, 'Let us make humankind in our image, according to our likeness'"; and Genesis 1:27: "So God created humankind in his image, in the image of God he created them; male and female he created them." The ambiguous fates of Ilia and Decker may be understood to suggest that both were transformed into new life-forms, with which the *Enterprise* crew could no longer communicate.

2. There's a wonderful if bizarre scene midway through the film *Beetlejuice*. Geena Davis and Alec Baldwin play recently deceased ghosts attempting to roust a family of pretentious, disaffected Manhattanites from their idyllic New England home. When their efforts meet with little success, they desperately consult a manual for the newly deceased. After drawing a door on the brick wall of their attic, they find themselves at a kind of social

service agency for the dead, seated in a waiting room with an assortment of weird-looking characters, including a person whose top and bottom halves are separate, a skeletal being smoking a cigarette, and a man with a shrunken head. Horrified and frightened, Geena Davis turns to Alec Baldwin and says, "Adam, is this what happens when you die?" The receptionist (no less weird looking, she appears to be wearing a bright-red wig, a strapless gown, and a Miss Argentina banner) is clearly irritated at their ignorance and replies sharply: "This is what happens when *you* die" (pointing at another recently deceased); "that is what happens when he dies, and that is what happens when they die. It's all very personal."

3. The show thus engages, in somewhat veiled form, an ancient Christian theological controversy about the fate of the dead and the nature of resurrection—whether in the body or not in the body. In 1 Corinthians 15:35–57, Paul offers a lengthy response to questions about the nature of the resurrected body: In a key passage (vv. 42–44), he writes: "So it is with the resurrection of the dead. What is sown is perishable, what is raised is imperishable. . . . It is sown a physical body, it is raised a spiritual body." Paul, in fact, goes on to suggest that some of his audience will not even experience death in the body at all, but experience a form of mysterious transformation (vv. 50–52), but that's yet another issue that Star Trek only rarely contemplates and, in any case, not in the kind of end-time scenario that Paul envisions.

4. Although the dilemmas of this episode are not wholly Christian, the show does contain subtle traces of Christian imagery. The reason the bodies are naked in the cavern is not because, as Chakotay imagines, the Vhnori bury their dead without clothing but rather because the spectral rupture must take only the body itself, leaving behind the burial cloths. As in *Star Trek III: The Search for Spock*, there is an interesting allusion to the narratives of the empty tomb in the Gospel of John (20:6–7) and in the Gospel of Luke (24:12), where the discovery of Jesus' burial cloths are taken as evidence of his (bodily) resurrection.

Chapter 6

1. Interestingly, the English word *salvation* is derived from the Latin verb *salvare*, "to save." In English, the word has two basic senses. The first is religious, and is overwhelmingly influenced by Christian theology in the specific sense of salvation as being saved from sin, thus becoming eligible for a heavenly reward. The other meaning is far more general: to be saved from danger or destruction. Since, in the United

Federation of Planets, people are not viewed as being stained by original sin (as Christianity holds) and other-worldly salvation is as obsolete as is religion in general, the first meaning doesn't much apply (although it is found in "alien" faiths such as those discussed in Chapter 5). But the second sense does apply: Star Trek is this-worldly, oriented to life in this universe as the only life that will exist. Star Trek characters are saving folks from danger and destruction in virtually every episode. They're not always successful, but it is what they do. Life is important. It must be preserved.

2. What we want to emphasize is that the image before our eyes makes sense from a Hindu perspective as an image of liberation, or salvation, while meaning in plot and characterization makes sense according to Star Trek forms of salvation. Odo has saved his people without sacrificing his integrity. He has also saved many Federation and allied warriors, as well as innocent Cardassians, from a bitter battle over Cardassia Prime, since without the Female Shapeshifter's surrender the war would have gone on. Odo has also fulfilled his obligations to his friends and is thus free to seek his destiny with his people. He is at peace, becoming at one. There are overtones of depth psychology here, particularly of the Jungian school. We suspect, too, that most of the creators of Star Trek were or are aware of the myth interpretations of Joseph Campbell as well, particularly his central thesis of the "hero's journey," a voyaging-out, the gaining of something of worth, and the return. We note that the hero's journey is primarily a male paradigm, despite Campbell's presentation of it as a universal one. Many have criticized the gender-specificity of Campbell's notion, as well as his claims for its universality. But this male quest scenario befits the masculinity of Odo's character.

3. The captain also interprets the symbolism of the artifact. The *naiskos*, with its host of interior figurines, represents the view of Kurlian civilization that "an individual was a community of individuals—the many voices inside the one." In the Jungian view, psychological growth includes spiritual dimensions and requires the ego to give up some of its autonomy as the center of the personality to the other "voices" within oneself. This relationship of individual and community is a central metaphor for the episode.

Index

Addiction, 199–200
Adonis, 23
Alaimo, Marc, 84
Alien abductions (contemporary), 30
Alternative universes/realities, 73, 154–157
Androgyny, 141
Angels, 17, 41, 71, 72, 74, 86, 99
Apollo, 1, 23, 24–25, 32, 183
Ardra, 31–32, 46, 49, 65, 67, 97
Armus, 62, 67
Arrogance, 226
Artifacts, 155, 210, 236(n3)
Asian traditions, 55, 120, 124, 125, 135, 148, 153, 154, 155, 219, 221, 222, 234(nn 4, 5)
Astrology, 123–124
Astrophysics, 233(n4)
Auberjonois, Rene, 193
Authentic/inauthentic existence, 20, 35, 36, 40, 182

Ba'al, 16, 18
Bajorans, 2, 98–101, 178, 179, 182, 185, 190, 193, 209, 232(n2, chap. 2), 232(nn 1, 2). *See also* Pah-wraiths; Prophets, Prophets of Bajor

Ba'ku race, 93–94, 95, 125, 203, 204
Beetlejuice, 234(n2)
Betazoid race, 109
Bhagavad Gita, 48
Bible, 16, 20, 41
    Book of Revelations, 48, 86
    Corinthians, 235(n3)
    Gospel of John, 36, 48, 49, 82, 164, 167, 235(n4)
    Gospel of Luke, 82, 164, 235(n4)
    Gospel of Mark, 88
    Gospel of Matthew, 109, 185
    See also Genesis
Binary opposites, 181
Body-mind/soul dualism, 102, 103, 177
Borg Collective, 72, 76–80, 195, 199, 200, 217, 218. *See also* Characters, Borg Queen
Buddhism, 55, 95, 101, 108, 109, 120, 125, 135, 148, 153, 175, 187–188, 191, 192, 199, 221

Caduceus, 144
Caissons, 35
Campbell, Joseph, 130, 236(n2)
Canada, 189